The Intrinsic
Need in the
Lord's Recovery–
Purification,
Education,
Reconstitution,
Separation,
Protection,
and Expression

Witness Lee

The
Holy
Word
for
Morning
Revival

Living Stream Ministry
Anaheim, CA • www.lsm.org

First Edition, December 2004.

ISBN 0-7363-2775-4

Published by

Living Stream Ministry
2431 W. La Palma Ave., Anaheim, CA 92801 U.S.A.
P. O. Box 2121, Anaheim, CA 92814 U.S.A.

Printed in the United States of America

04 05 06 07 08 09 10 / 10 9 8 7 6 5 4 3 2 1

Contents

Preface

1. This book is intended as an aid to believers in developing a daily time of morning revival with the Lord in His word. At the same time, it provides a limited review of the Thanksgiving weekend conference held in San Francisco, California, November 25-28, 2004. The subject of the conference was "The Intrinsic Need in the Lord's Recovery—Purification, Education, Reconstitution, Separation, Protection, and Expression." Through intimate contact with the Lord in His word, the believers can be constituted with life and truth and thereby equipped to prophesy in the meetings of the church unto the building up of the Body of Christ.

2. The content of this book is taken primarily from the conference message outlines, the text and footnotes of the Recovery Version of the Bible, selections from the writings of Witness Lee and Watchman Nee, and *Hymns,* all of which are published by Living Stream Ministry.

3. The book is divided into weeks. One conference message is covered per week. Each week presents first the message outline, followed by six daily portions, a hymn, and then some space for writing. The message outline has been divided into days, corresponding to the six daily portions. Each daily portion covers certain points and begins with a section entitled "Morning Nourishment." This section contains selected verses and a short reading that can provide rich spiritual nourishment through intimate fellowship with the Lord. The "Morning Nourishment" is followed by a section entitled "Today's Reading," a longer portion of ministry related to the day's main points. Each day's portion concludes with a short list of references for further reading and some space for the saints to make notes concerning their spiritual inspiration, enlightenment, and enjoyment to serve as a reminder of what they have received of the Lord that day.

4. The space provided at the end of each week is for composing a short prophecy. This prophecy can be composed by

considering all of our daily notes, the "harvest" of our inspirations during the week, and preparing a main point with some sub-points to be spoken in the church meetings for the organic building up of the Body of Christ.

5. Following the last week in this volume, we have provided a reading schedule for the New Testament Recovery Version with footnotes. This schedule is arranged so that one can read through the complete New Testament Recovery Version with footnotes in two years.

6. As a practical aid to the saints' feeding on the Word throughout the day, we have provided verse cards at the end of the volume, which correspond to each day's scripture reading. These may be cut out and carried along as a source of spiritual enlightenment and nourishment in the saint's daily lives.

7. The conference outlines were compiled by Living Stream Ministry from the writings of Witness Lee and Watchman Nee. The outlines, footnotes, and references in the Recovery Version of the Bible were written by Witness Lee. All of the other references cited in this publication are from the ministry of Witness Lee and Watchman Nee.

Thanksgiving Weekend
Conference
(November 25-28, 2004)

General Subject:

The Intrinsic Need in the Lord's Recovery—
Purification, Education, Reconstitution,
Separation, Protection, and Expression

Banners:

In the Lord's recovery,
we need to be purified of every kind of mixture
in order to become pure
in heart, in conscience, and in spirit.

God's intention is to reconstitute us
with Himself so that we may become
His corporate expression, the Body of Christ
consummating in the New Jerusalem.

By living in our spirit and
eating Christ as the hidden manna,
we can overcome the world
to become God's building.

Today in His recovery the Lord is working
to restore the normal condition
of Christ within the proper church
as His expression.

Purification

Scripture Reading: Ezra 9:1-15; Neh. 13:23-30a; Matt. 5:8; Rev. 21:18b, 21b; 22:4

Day 1

I. **The Lord's recovery is unique, and in the recovery we must be purified of every kind of mixture:**

A. Babylon is a mixture of the things of God with the things of idols, and the principle of Babylon is the principle of mixing the things of man with the Word of God and the things of the flesh with the things of the Spirit (2 Chron. 36:6-7; Ezra 1:11; Rev. 17:3-5):

1. Anything that is a part of Babylon is abominable in the sight of God, and anything Babylonian gives Satan the ground to defeat the people of God (Josh. 7:1-21).

2. God hates the principle of Babylon more than anything else; only when we judge everything Babylonian in us can we confess that we too hate the principle of Babylon.

B. Before Ezra arrived, there was mixture among God's recovered people, but he purified the recovery by causing "the holy seed" to be separated from anything heathen (Ezra 9:1-15):

1. The Lord's recovery must be pure and without mixture; thus, we need Ezras and Nehemiahs to carry out a purifying work (Neh. 13:23-30a).

2. In the local churches, we must be purified from all mixture (2 Tim. 2:21).

C. In Acts 21 and in the book of James, there is mixture, because James was a mixed person:

1. Acts 21 exposes the terrible mixture in the church in Jerusalem; this mixture was a cause for God's sending Titus and the Roman army to destroy the city of Jerusalem, including the temple (Matt. 24:1-2; 22:7).

2. James mixed the Old Testament with the New Testament, the new dispensation with the old, the new people of God with the old, and the new man with the old man (James 1:1, 17-18; 2:1-4, 8-12; 3:2; 4:11-12; 5:10-11).

Day 2

D. A great problem among God's children is the mixture of the self with the spirit (Heb. 4:12):

1. This mixture disqualifies many from serving God, for in their spirit there is much mixture, which is displeasing to God (2 Tim. 1:3).

2. The spirit in our innermost part is pure and undefiled; however, when the spirit comes forth and passes through the soul and the body, it may become contaminated by filthiness and corruption (2 Cor. 7:1).

3. Dealing with the spirit emphasizes dealing with impure motives and intentions and other mixtures within us (1 Thes. 5:23; 2 Tim. 1:7).

Day 3

II. **We need to be pure in heart, in conscience, and in spirit:**

A. Those who are pure in heart will see God (Matt. 5:8; Job 42:5; Rev. 22:4):

1. To be pure in heart is to be single in purpose, to have the single goal of accomplishing God's will for God's glory (1 Cor. 10:31).

2. A pure heart is a heart that takes the Lord as the unique goal (1 Tim. 1:5; 2 Tim. 2:22; Psa. 73:1).

3. In the New Testament sense, to see God is to gain God, and to gain God is to receive God in His element, life, and nature in order to be constituted with God, to become one with God, to become a part of God, and to become God in life and nature but not in the Godhead (Matt. 5:8; Rev. 22:4).

4. We should be pure in heart and single for the Lord's recovery; only then will we be a

help to the recovery (1 Tim. 1:5; 2 Tim. 2:22; 1 Pet. 1:22).

B. We need to have not only a good conscience but also a pure conscience (Acts 23:1; 24:16; 1 Tim. 3:9; 2 Tim. 1:3):

   1. A good conscience is a conscience without offense toward God and man (Acts 23:1; 24:16).

Day 4 & Day 5

   2. A pure conscience is a conscience purified of any mixture; such a conscience testifies that, like Paul, we are seeking only God and His will (2 Tim. 1:3).

C. The first qualification in the work is purity of spirit (2 Cor. 6:4a, 6):

   1. It is very difficult to find a person whose spirit is pure (7:1).

   2. Pureness is the prerequisite in the leadership and a basic condition of our service (1 Tim. 3:9; 1:5):

      a. It is unusual to find a pure motive in what touches the Lord's work or His church; the problem of mixture is the greatest problem among workers (2 Tim. 1:3; 1 Tim. 3:9).

      b. Impureness is often the source of misunderstanding and suspicion (Titus 1:15).

   3. We need to deal completely with all the mixture in our spirit so that when our spirit is released, it will not be dangerous or cause trouble to others.

   4. If we want to be used by God, our spirit must be released, and our spirit must be pure (2 Cor. 6:4a, 6).

Day 6   III. **The city of New Jerusalem is pure gold, like clear glass, and the street of the city is pure gold, like transparent glass (Rev. 21:18b, 21b):**

A. Gold signifies the nature of God; the city's being pure gold indicates that the city is of the divine nature and takes the divine nature as its element (v. 18b).

B. The pure gold of the street and the city is like clear glass, signifying that the entire city is transparent and not in the least opaque (v. 21b):

1. If we take God's nature as our unique way, we will be pure, without any mixture, and transparent, without any opaqueness.

2. If we are infused and saturated with the life-giving Spirit, our inner being will become transparent and crystal clear (2 Cor. 5:21).

C. If we want to have the real church life, the church herself must be pure gold, that is, altogether of the divine nature; here we need the work of the cross to purge us and to purify us (Rev. 1:11, 20).

D. The difference between apostate Christendom and the genuine church is that one is a mixture and the other is pure; the local churches, like the New Jerusalem, should be crystal clear, without any mixture (22:1).

Morning Nourishment

Eph. **That He would grant you...to be strengthened with**
3:16 **power through His Spirit into the inner man.**
4:22 **That you put off, as regards your former manner of**
life, the old man, which is being corrupted...
24 **And put on the new man, which was created accord-**
ing to God in righteousness and holiness of the reality.
1 Cor. **...A soulish man does not receive the things of the Spirit**
2:14 **of God, for they are foolishness to him and he is not able**
to know *them* because they are discerned spiritually.

Under God's sovereignty, there are the Old Testament and the New Testament with the old dispensation and the new dispensation. God has two peoples: the old people, Israel, and the new people, the church. Also, there are the old man and the new man. When we speak concerning the Epistle of James, we must realize these four pairs of items....I consider the apostle James as the top mixer. He mixed the New Testament with the Old Testament, the new dispensation with the old, the new people of God with the old, and the new man with the old man. The debate on the book of James cannot be resolved unless one sees these factors. (*Crystallization-study of the Epistle of James*, p. 4)

Today's Reading

The New Testament tells us we have to put off the old man and put on the new man (Eph. 4:22-24). It also tells us that we have to deny the self, which is the corrupted soul, the old man (Matt. 16:24). Then we need God's strengthening to strengthen our entire being into the inner man, which is the new man (Eph. 3:16). Hebrews 4:12 tells us that the sharp word of God operates to divide our soul from our spirit. This is a base for our study on James.

The stress of the Epistle of James is Christian perfection. According to history and according to James's writing, there are different perfections on different levels in different ages. Job 1:1 says that Job was a perfect man....In Philippians 3:6 Paul said that as to the righteousness of the law he had become blameless, perfect....Job's perfection was before the law, and Saul's perfection was under the law. Now we have James's perfection, but in what age? His perfection is not only in the age of the law but also in the age of grace. James is a person with one foot in the age of law and the other in the age of grace. Thus, he is one person standing in two ages. This is the perfection of James, but this is not the genuine Christian perfection revealed in the entire New Testament....The genuine Christian perfection is purely under the absolute grace of God....The Christian perfection stressed by James was under both the law and grace, by both the old, natural man and the new, regenerated man. This is a mixture.

In his teaching of the Jewish believers concerning the virtues of Christian perfection, James did not warn them, as Paul did in dealing with the Corinthian believers (1 Cor. 2:14), that the virtues of Christian perfection should only be produced and carried out by the regenerated persons and not by the natural persons. Here a hidden mixture is implied: a mixture of the regenerated persons, in their regenerated humanity mingled with divinity, with the natural persons in their fallen humanity, in the producing and carrying out of the virtues of Christian perfection. In the church as the organic Body of Christ, everything must be done by the regenerated persons, in whom is God's delight, and nothing should be done by the natural persons, for whom is God's condemnation.

By the thorough destruction of the city of Jerusalem with its temple in A.D. 70, God terminated the Jewish religious service to Him, symbolized by the temple, and the nation of the Jews, symbolized by the city of Jerusalem....This was prophesied by the Lord Jesus....By the destruction of Jerusalem God also wiped out all the vague situation and mixtures among the believers caused by James's vague vision and mistake and separated the believers from the Jewish people and anything Jewish. (*Crystallization-study of the Epistle of James*, pp. 4-5, 72, 75-76)

Further Reading: Crystallization-study of the Epistle of James, msgs. 1, 3, 6-7; The Glorious Church, ch. 5; The Living and Practical Way to Enjoy Christ, ch. 7; The Recovery of God's House and God's City, chs. 3, 7-8

Enlightenment and inspiration: _____

_____

_____

_____

Morning Nourishment

Heb. **For the word of God is living and operative and**
4:12 **sharper than any two-edged sword, and piercing**
even to the dividing of soul and spirit and of joints
and marrow, and able to discern the thoughts and
intentions of the heart.

2 Cor. **Therefore since we have these promises, beloved,**
7:1 **let us cleanse ourselves from all defilement of flesh**
and of spirit, perfecting holiness in the fear of God.

1 Thes. **And the God of peace Himself sanctify you wholly,**
5:23 **and may your spirit and soul and body be pre-**
served complete, without blame, at the coming of
our Lord Jesus Christ.

Though we have said that the spirit must be clean, yet the spirit itself is not actually filthy. Indeed, 2 Corinthians 7:1 says to "cleanse ourselves from all defilement of...spirit," but this defilement is not of the spirit itself, but a defilement effected by the soul and body.

If the spirit itself is not filthy, why does it sometimes manifest itself in an unclean and improper manner? It is because the spirit must pass through many of our inward parts when it comes forth. Within the inward parts is filthiness, so that when the spirit passes through them it is defiled, and thus the filthiness is brought forth also. Therefore when the spirit is released and manifested, it exhibits certain defiled and improper conditions.

Since the defilement of the spirit is due to the passage of the spirit (which includes the purpose of the heart, motive, aim, intention, etc.), then dealing with the spirit is not dealing with the spirit itself, but with the passage of the spirit, that is, with the purpose of the heart, motive, aim, intention, etc. (*The Experience of Life,* pp. 285-286, 289)

Today's Reading

Whenever we are about to act or speak, not only do we need to inquire whether what we are about to do is right or wrong, good or bad, but we must also discern whether or not our inner intention is clean, our motive pure, and our aim wholly for God. Is there any selfish purpose behind our action? Is there any self-inclination? This kind of dealing is dealing with the spirit.

For example, suppose a certain brother has a controversy with you, which causes you to be very angry and disgusted. When you mention him to others, although outwardly you speak lightly as if nothing really matters, nevertheless your words cause others to sense a spirit of condemnation and anger. One day, perhaps during a meeting or while in prayer, you receive mercy from the Lord and realize that since the Lord has forgiven you, you must certainly forgive your brother. At this time, from your deepest being, you deal thoroughly with your unforgiving purpose of heart and intention. Later, when you mention this brother to others, although you touch the controversial matter of the past, your spirit is undisturbed and upright. At this time, not only does your spirit come forth, but it comes forth cleanly without any other intention.

Since the passage of the spirit includes every part of our being, we need to deal with every part of our being when dealing with the spirit. This kind of dealing is deeper and more delicate than the various dealings mentioned before....Beginning with dealing with sin, every step of the dealings becomes deeper and finer as we go on. When we come to dealing with the natural constitution, we are being dealt with completely within and without. The only part remaining is the mixture coming forth with the spirit. When we have the spirit dealt with and cleansed from all mixtures, so that not only does the spirit come forth, but it comes forth as a clean, pure, and upright spirit, then our whole being is completely and thoroughly dealt with. Therefore, following this, we obtain the filling of the Spirit. When all the elements of our old creation have been completely dealt with, then the Holy Spirit can possess and fill our whole being. (*The Experience of Life,* pp. 285-286, 289-291)

Further Reading: The Experience of Life, ch. 13

Enlightenment and inspiration: _____

_____

_____

_____

Morning Nourishment

Acts And Paul...said, Men, brothers, I have conducted my-
23:1 self in all good conscience before God until this day.
24:16 Because of this I also exercise myself to always have a
      conscience without offense toward God and men.
2 Tim. I thank God, whom I serve from *my* forefathers in a
1:3 pure conscience...
1 Tim. Holding the mystery of the faith in a pure conscience.
3:9

The conscience is the leading part of our spirit. If our conscience is wrong, we can never have a proper spirit. Moreover,
we can never even exercise our spirit. In fact, if our conscience is
wrong, our spirit is dead! Therefore, before we can properly exercise our spirit, we must first have a *good* conscience. Then, we
also need a *pure* conscience.

However, we may have a good conscience which does not condemn us in any matter, but it may not be pure. A pure conscience
means that we are only seeking God and His will. Many times,
we are seeking God, but we are also seeking something *besides
God!* It may not be anything sinful, it may even be something
good, but it is not God Himself. Therefore, our heart is not pure,
for it is not seeking God alone. Since our heart is not pure, our
conscience also is not pure. When our heart is single, pure and
seeking only God, our conscience then becomes pure. But when
our heart seeks something besides God, it will influence our conscience. At this time, we may have a good conscience, yet it is not
pure. (*The Stream*, vol. 5, no. 1, pp. 10-11)

Today's Reading

Even though we may have a good conscience, if we lack a pure
conscience, we can never serve God in an adequate way. Our conscience must first be good; then secondly, it must be pure. Many
times we meet a good brother who really loves the Lord. Although
he is for God, we soon discover that he is also for the work of the
gospel. This means he is pursuing something else besides God
Himself. Of course, he is not doing anything sinful; consequently,
he does not have a bad conscience. His conscience is good. But he

is taking more care of the gospel work than the Lord Himself. His conscience does not condemn him because his gospel work for the Lord is very good. But his difficulty is that his gospel work is a substitute for the Lord in his life. It is something *of* the Lord, yet it is not the *Lord*. This brother may have a good conscience, but he could never have a pure conscience.

Paul said, "God, whom I serve...in a pure conscience." It means that he was seeking after nothing else but God Himself. How important it is that we have such a pure conscience!

If we are going to have a pure conscience, we must first have a pure heart. To be pure means to be single unto God. In other words, our mind considers *nothing* but the Lord, our emotion loves *nothing* but the Lord and our will chooses *nothing* but the Lord. Then we will have a pure heart, seeking only the Lord. A pure conscience must first have a pure heart.

Let us check ourselves. Is our mind fully and wholly occupied with nothing but the Lord? Does our emotion simply, wholly and fully love the Lord more than anything else? Is our will completely for God? If we are honest, we will immediately say, "No, I am not so pure." Our mind wanders, our emotion loves many other things and our will is unstable. Only when these parts are pure will we have a pure heart, and when our heart is pure, our conscience will then be pure. This pure conscience is very vital to the exercise of the spirit.

If our conscience is not pure, our spirit can never be strong. Our spirit is weak because a certain condemnation exists within our conscience, which indicates that we are not so pure and single unto the Lord. We are seeking something other than the Lord, although it may not be sinful. Deeply within our conscience, there is a very fine condemnation. It is not very rough or coarse, but a certain kind of condemnation, so tender and fine, always telling us that we are not fully for the Lord. Such condemnation weakens our spirit. (*The Stream,* vol. 5, no. 1, pp. 11-12)

Further Reading: The Stream, vol. 5, no. 1; *Life-study of Job,* msg. 30

Enlightenment and inspiration: _____

_____

_____

_____

Morning Nourishment

1 Tim. But the end of the charge is love *out of* a pure heart and
1:5 *out of* a good conscience and out of unfeigned faith.
Titus All things are pure to the pure; yet to those who are de-
1:15 filed and unbelieving nothing is pure, but both their
mind and their conscience are defiled.

The problem of mixture is the biggest problem among workers.
We often touch life in the brothers, but also touch death. We touch
God in the brothers, but also touch their self. We touch a spirit of
meekness, but also touch a stubborn self. We find the Holy Spirit in
them, but also find the flesh in them. When they stand up to speak,
others sense a mixed spirit, an impure spirit. If God intends for us
to serve Him in the ministry of the word and if we have to speak for
God, we have to ask for grace. We have to say, "God, work in me.
Break my outer man, tear it down, and separate it from the inner
man." If we have not experienced this deliverance, we will express
our outer man unconsciously every time we open our mouth. There
is no way for us to hide it. As soon as the word goes out, the spirit
goes out as well. We are the kind of person we are; we cannot pre-
tend. If we want to be used by God, our spirit must be released, and
this spirit must be pure. In order for us to be pure, our outer man
must be destroyed. If our outer man is not destroyed, we will carry
our own cargo with us when we serve as ministers of the word. The
Lord's name will suffer loss, not on account of our lack of life, but on
account of our mixture. The Lord's name will suffer, and the church
will suffer as well. (Watchman Nee, *The Breaking of the Outer Man
and the Release of the Spirit,* p. 82)

Today's Reading

Among Christians a pure motive is a treasure. It is rarer than a
diamond. In my "practice of medicine" for over a half a century, I
have surely known what "sicknesses" people have. It is unusual to
find a pure motive in what touches the Lord's work or His church.

Impureness in the church life and in the Lord's work is the basic
killer. It kills everything, including you, if you are impure. As long
as you have impurity in your motive, you are the first victim of this

impureness. This is not a threat; it is a warning, firstly to myself. Only the Lord knows how fearful and trembling I have been for many years lest I be impure in making a decision concerning certain things.

My conscience allows me to ask you brothers: Is there any hint of impurity regarding the church and the Lord's work as far as I myself am concerned? I have been with you for twenty years. Tonight I stand before you, about a hundred people, to say that it's hard for you to find anything of the church and the Lord's work related to me that is impure. Brothers, this is the only reason that the Lord's blessing, not in prosperity but in life, is here. And it is because of this that I can speak boldly. My conscience does not have even a small hole. In other things I dare not say; but in this matter of pureness I have a conscience without offense.

The prerequisite...in responsibility, in the eldership, in the leadership, is pureness. The coordination needs pureness. If you are short of this, regardless of how careful you are, you will have trouble again and again. In the church life, things are always happening. If you are not pure in your motive, you will be entangled either by this trouble or by the next one. It is unavoidable. By the same token, if you are pure, no trouble will entangle you.

To offend others comes from the flesh. Fear of offending others is also of the flesh. In the world, say, in a corporation, people are very careful not to offend each other, because the world is filled with impurity. If this is true of the church also, we are no more the church. In the church there should be nothing but pureness in every avenue, every corner.

It is when we are impure that we become suspicious. We become detectives to spy out the meaning behind what others say. If we are pure in our motive, we do not have such a thought. We are on another globe, taking others' words in a simple way. (*Practical Talks to the Elders*, pp. 26-28)

Further Reading: The Breaking of the Outer Man and the Release of the Spirit, ch. 7; *Practical Talks to the Elders*, chs. 1-2

Enlightenment and inspiration: _____

_____

_____

_____

Morning Nourishment

2 Cor. ...In everything we commend ourselves as ministers
6:4, 6 of God,...in pureness, in knowledge, in long-suffering,
in kindness, in a holy spirit, in unfeigned love.
Heb. For the word of God is living and operative and sharper
4:12 than any two-edged sword, and piercing even to the
dividing of soul and spirit,...and able to discern the
thoughts and intentions of the heart.

A problem among God's children is the mixture of the soul
with the spirit. Whenever their spirit is released, their soul is released as well. It is hard to find a person whose spirit is pure. With
many people this purity is lacking. It is this mixture that disqualifies them from being used by God. The first qualification in the
work is a purity of the spirit, not a measure of power. Many people
hope to have great power, yet they pay no attention to purity in
the spirit. Although they have the power to build, they are short
in purity. As a result their work is bound for destruction. On the
one hand, they build with power. On the other hand, they destroy
with their impurity. They demonstrate God's power, yet at the
same time their spirit is a mixed spirit. (Watchman Nee, *The
Breaking of the Outer Man and the Release of the Spirit*, p. 79)

Today's Reading

Some people think that as long as they receive power from
God, everything that they have will be sublimated and be taken
up by God for His service. But this will never happen. Whatever
belongs to the outer man will forever belong to the outer man. The
more we know God, the more we will treasure purity over power.
We cherish this purity. This purity is different from spiritual
power, and it is free from any contamination of the outer man. If a
man has never experienced any dealing in his outer man, it is impossible to expect the power that issues from him to be pure. He
cannot assume that just because he has spiritual power and has
produced some results in his work that he is free to mix his self
with his spirit. If he does this, he will become a problem. This, in
fact, is a sin.

Many young brothers and sisters know that the gospel is the power of God. But when they preach the gospel, they add in their own cleverness, frivolity, jokes, and personal feelings. Others can sense God's power with them, but at the same time they also sense the self. The preachers themselves may not feel anything, but the pure ones immediately will sense the presence of mixture.

Our greatest problem is our mixture. Hence, God has to work on us to break our outer man as well as to remove our mixture. God is breaking us step by step so that our outer man will no longer be whole. After our outer man is battered once, ten, twenty times, we will be broken and our hard outer shell before God will be gone. But what should we do with the mixture of the outer man in our spirit? This requires another work—the work of purging. This work is carried out not only through the discipline of the Spirit, but also through the revelation of the Spirit. The way to purge mixture is different from the way to break the outer man. The way to purge mixture is often through revelation. Therefore, we find God dealing with us in two ways. One is the breaking of the outer man, and the other is the separation of the outer man from the spirit. One comes through the discipline of the Holy Spirit, and the other is the result of the revelation of the Holy Spirit.

Breaking and separation are our two different needs. Yet there is a strong relationship between the two, and it is impossible to disassociate the two altogether. The outer man needs to be broken before the spirit can be released. But when the spirit is released, it must not be mixed with the sentiments and characteristics of the outer man. It must not carry any element that comes from man. This is not merely a matter of the release of the spirit, but a matter of the purity and quality of the spirit....The issue is not whether the spirit is released, but whether the spirit is pure. (Watchman Nee, *The Breaking of the Outer Man and the Release of the Spirit,* pp. 79-81)

Further Reading: The Breaking of the Outer Man and the Release of the Spirit, ch. 7

Enlightenment and inspiration: _____

_____

_____

Morning Nourishment

2 Cor. Him who did not know sin He made sin on our
5:21 behalf that we might become the righteousness
      of God in Him.
Rev. The mystery of...the seven golden lampstands:...
1:20 The seven lampstands are the seven churches.
21:18 ...And the city was pure gold, like clear glass.
22:1 And he showed me a river of water of life, bright
      as crystal, proceeding out of the throne of God and
      of the Lamb in the middle of its street.

As a result of experiencing the Spirit living and working within us, we become righteous [2 Cor. 5:21]. Spontaneously our inner being is transparent, crystal clear, and we know the heart of God. Immediately, without effort, we know the mind of the Lord and have a clear understanding concerning His will and work. Then what we do is according to the Lord's mind and will. This is righteousness.

If you are infused and saturated by the life-giving Spirit, your inner being will become transparent. Then you will know what is in the Lord's mind. You will also understand what the will of the Lord is. Spontaneously, you will be in His will and do His will. As a result, you become right with Him. Moreover, you will realize how you should act toward others and even how you should deal with your material possessions. Then you will become a righteous person, one who is right in small things as well as in great things, one who is right with God, with others, and with himself. This is a person who expresses God, for his righteousness is the image of God, God expressed. (*Life-study of 2 Corinthians*, pp. 242-243)

Today's Reading

The pure gold of the unique street in the New Jerusalem is "like transparent glass," signifying without any opaqueness [Rev. 21:21]. The golden street is crystal clear, without any opaqueness. This indicates that if we take God's nature as our unique way, we will be pure, without any mixture, and transparent without opaqueness. (*The Conclusion of the New Testament*, p. 2734)

The whole city itself is gold. In all the Scriptures, gold signifies the divine nature, the nature of God the Father. The city itself is pure gold without any mixture (Rev. 21:18b). This indicates that the church must be one hundred percent of God; it must be absolutely of the divine nature. Today among Christians, however, the church is a mixture with some part of the divine nature and some part of the fallen human nature. If we want to have the real church life, the church herself must be pure gold, that is, altogether of the divine nature. Here we need the work of the cross to purify us and to purge us.

Being pure is different from being clean.... [Most would think] that to be cleansed [is] good enough. However,...we still need to be purified, just as pure gold is purified to contain no mixture and to be transparent....A dear brother may be nice, gentle, and clean but still have a mixture. He is not transparent but opaque. He is nice and clean, but you cannot see through him. When I am surrounded by brothers who have a mixture, I say, "Lord, deliver me. I am in a 'prison cell,' and every side is opaque." The more such brothers talk, the more they are in darkness, even if they are clean persons. To be clean is one thing, but to be pure and transparent is another. Sometimes you may meet a saint in the Lord, whom you sense is not only clean but also transparent, like clear glass. I had a history with Brother Watchman Nee for over thirty years. Within all those years, every time I met him I had the sense that he was a transparent man. When I sat before him, I could see through him. Every time he stood on the platform to give a message, the audience could sense that he was transparent. When he opened his mouth to speak only a few words, you could sense that everything became transparent. Brothers and sisters, we should be clear that simply to be clean is not enough. We need to be purified by the death of the Lord on the cross. (*The Central Thought of God,* pp. 122-123)

Further Reading: Life-study of 2 Corinthians, msg. 27; The Conclusion of the New Testament, msg. 262; The Central Thought of God, ch. 13

Enlightenment and inspiration: _____

_____

_____

_____

Hymns, #744

1 In dealings with the Lord as life
      We need a proper heart,
   That of His riches, in His grace,
      We fully may take part.

2 We need a heart in all things pure,
      With mind both sound and clear,
   To understand His mind and heart
      In trembling and in fear.

3 We need a fervent, loving heart,
      A heart on fire with love,
   With an emotion filled with zeal
      For Him, all else above.

4 We need a true, obedient heart,
      With a submissive will,
   A will made pliable, yet strong,
      God's purpose to fulfill.

5 We need a heart condemning not,
      In all things right with God;
   A heart which has a conscience purged
      And covered with the blood.

6 Lord, grant us such a heart as this,
      Forever fixed on Thee,
   That of Thyself we may partake
      And Thy true fulness be.

Composition for prophecy with main point and sub-points: _____

_____
_____
_____
_____
_____
_____
_____
_____
_____
_____
_____
_____
_____
_____
_____
_____
_____
_____
_____
_____
_____
_____
_____
_____
_____
_____
_____
_____
_____
_____
_____
_____
_____
_____
_____
_____
_____

Education

Scripture Reading: Ezra 7:6, 10-12, 21; Neh. 8:1-13; 12:26

Day 1   I. **In the Lord's recovery, we need Ezras to constitute God's people by educating them with the truth so that they may be God's testimony, His corporate expression, on earth (Neh. 8:1-8, 13; 2 Tim. 2:2, 15; 1 Tim. 3:15):**
   A. Ezra was a priest and also a scribe; thus, he was not a letter-scribe but a priestly scribe (Ezra 7:6, 11-12, 21; Neh. 8:1-2, 8-9, 11-12; 12:26).
   B. Ezra was skilled in the law of God, which is linked to God's economy (Ezra 7:6, 10-12):
      1. God's economy is God becoming a man that man may become God in life and in nature but not in the Godhead to produce the organic Body of Christ, which will consummate in the New Jerusalem (Rom. 8:3; 1:3-4; 12:4-5; Rev. 21:2).
      2. The center, reality, and goal of God's economy is Christ (Col. 1:15-18).
      3. The law is linked to God's economy because the law was given as God's testimony—God's portrait, God's image (Exo. 25:16, 21):
         a. The living law of God as God's testimony dwells in Christ, making Him the testimony of God (Col. 2:9).
         b. As God's testimony, the law is a type of Christ, the image of God, who is God's portrait and testimony (1:15).
         c. In typology, to keep the law means to express God (1 Cor. 10:31).
         d. Those who have the living of a God-man bear the image of God; they are a portrait of God and even a duplication of God (Phil. 1:19-21a; 2 Cor. 3:18; Rom. 8:4, 9).
Day 2   C. Ezra spoke what had been spoken by Moses (Ezra 7:6; Neh. 8:14; 2 Pet. 1:12).

D. The priests and the Levites were gathered to Ezra the scribe in order to gain insight into the words of the law; in Nehemiah 8:13 *insight* refers to apprehending the intrinsic significance.

Day 3 II. In the Lord's recovery we need Ezras, priestly teachers who contact God, who are saturated with God, who are one with God, who are mingled with God, who are filled with God, and who are skillful in the Word of God; this is the kind of person who is qualified to be a teacher in the recovery (Matt. 13:52; 2 Cor. 3:5-6; 1 Tim. 2:7; 2 Tim. 1:11):

A. The Lord Jesus taught the people in order to bring them out of the satanic darkness into the divine light (Mark 6:6; cf. Acts 26:18):

1. Man's fall into sin broke his fellowship with God, making all men ignorant of the knowledge of God, with such ignorance issuing in darkness and death (Eph. 4:17-18).

2. The Lord as the light of the world came as a great light to shine on the people who were sitting in the shadow of death (John 8:12; Matt. 4:12-16).

3. The Lord's teaching released the word of light that those in darkness and death might receive the light of life (John 1:4).

B. Teaching equals revelation, which is the opening of the veil (1 Tim. 2:7; Eph. 3:3-4, 9):

1. To teach is to roll away the veil; as we are teaching others, we should be taking away the veil so that they may see something of the Triune God.

2. When we speak something in the church meeting, our speaking should be the rolling away of the veil; this means that our teaching should present a revelation (1 Tim. 4:6, 11, 16).

C. The kind of person we are determines the kind of Bible we have (1 Cor. 2:11-16):

    1. Our understanding of the Bible is always according to what we are (2 Cor. 3:12-16).

    2. What we see in the Bible and what the Bible is to us depend upon what kind of person we are (John 5:39-40; Matt. 5:8; 6:22-24, 33; Luke 11:34-36).

Day 4   **III. The greatest need we must meet is to bring the saints in the Lord's recovery into the truth to carry the recovery on (1 Tim. 2:4; 2 Tim. 2:2, 15):**

  A. The recovery has the highest truth—the truth that is the consummation of the truths recovered during the past centuries (1 Tim. 2:4; 2 Tim. 2:2, 15):

    1. We have both the objective truths and the subjective truths in the Holy Scriptures (Luke 24:39; 1 Cor. 15:45b; Rom. 8:34, 10; Col. 3:1; 1:27).

Day 5   2. In our study of the Bible, we should not merely pay attention to the "branches" but go deeply into the "roots" and the "trunk."

    3. We need to see the crystallized significances of the steps of God's economy and of the Body of Christ (John 1:14; 1 Cor. 15:45b; Eph. 1:22-23; 4:4-6).

    4. We need to refute and correct the defects and errors of traditional Christian theology (Col. 1:25; 2 Tim. 2:15, 25).

  B. To be constituted with the truth is to have the truth wrought into us to become our intrinsic being, our organic constitution (2 John 2):

    1. The intrinsic element of the divine revelation must be wrought into and constituted into our being (Col. 3:16).

    2. Once the truth gets into us through our understanding, it remains in our memory, and then we retain the truth in our memory, causing us to have an accumulation of the truth (1 Pet. 1:13; 2 Pet. 1:15; 3:1).

3. After the truth gets into our memory, it becomes a constant and long-term nourishment; then we have an accumulation of the
truth, and we are under the constant nourishment (Col. 3:16, 4; 1 Tim. 4:6).

C. We must learn to use the new language of the
new culture in the divine and mystical realm
(Neh. 13:23-24; 1 Cor. 2:12-13; John 16:12-15).

Day 6   D. All the saints in the Lord's recovery should be
trained in the divine revelation (2 Tim. 2:2, 15):

1. Nearly all the crucial revelations in the
Bible have been covered in the ministry of
Brother Nee and Brother Lee; we should
pay our attention to these pure and healthy
things and not waste our time collecting
"poisonous gourds" (2 Kings 4:38-41).

2. We all need to be helped through the
Life-studies and the Recovery Version with
the footnotes to see the intrinsic significance of the word of the Bible (Neh. 8:8, 13).

Morning Nourishment

Col.   ...The Son of His love,...who is the image of the invis-
1:13, 15   ible God...
Phil.   According to my earnest expectation and hope that
1:20-21   in nothing I will be put to shame, but with all boldness, as always, even now Christ will be magnified in
my body, whether through life or through death. For
to me, to live is Christ...

The Ten Commandments were called the testimony of God
(Exo. 25:16). As the testimony of God the Ten Commandments
are a picture, a portrait, of God. We may say that the law is a
photograph of God. A particular law is always a portrait of the
person who makes that law....The law of God is a portrait of
God....The more we consider the law of God, the more we realize
that this Lawmaker, this Legislator, must be One who is full of
love and light, One who is holy and righteous.

Because the law is God's portrait, God's image, it is called
God's testimony. The Ark in which the law was placed was
called the Ark of the Testimony (Exo. 25:22). (*Life-study of 1 &
2 Chronicles,* pp. 74-75)

Today's Reading

Based upon the fact that the law is the testimony of God, a picture of God, we may say that the law is also a type of Christ. How
can the law be a type of Christ? The law is a type of Christ because
Christ is God's portrait, God's picture, God's image (Col. 1:15).

Now we need to see how the law is linked to God's economy....
In His economy God chose Israel, established them as a people,
formed them as a nation, and gave them the law. How can we
link this with God's economy? God's economy is God becoming a
man that man may become God in life and in nature (but not in
the Godhead) to produce the organic Body of Christ, which will
consummate in the New Jerusalem. Christ is the center, the reality, and the goal of God's economy. The law seems to have nothing to do with such an economy. How, then, can the law be linked
to God's economy? The law is linked to God's economy because

the law was given as God's portrait, God's picture, God's image, and God's testimony. As God's testimony the law is a type of Christ, who, being the image of God, is God's portrait, God's picture, God's testimony.

God charged Israel to keep the law. In typology, to keep the law means to express God. Keeping the law...is the living of a God-man. Those who have the living of a God-man bear the image of God. They are a portrait of God and even a duplication of God.

The situation of today's world is utterly different from this. In the world we see not the life of a God-man but murder, adultery, fornication, stealing, lying, and coveting. Who tells the truth today? It is common for people to lie in a court of law in order to get money and then to boast about their lying. Many compete with others in business or at school because of their coveting. All the competitive ones are covetous. Some will even kill to get what they covet. Therefore, instead of being full of God-men, the earth is full of "scorpions."

Because we are short of the God-man living, we need a real revival. The children of Israel had only an outward law, but today we have something much stronger and much higher than the law. We have the all-inclusive, life-giving, compounded, consummated Spirit in us, who is the bountiful supply of the Spirit of Jesus Christ (Phil. 1:19). We need to live Christ by the bountiful supply of the Spirit of Jesus Christ (vv. 20-21a).

We have such a Spirit within us, but what do we live and how do we live? Do we live Christ? In the church meetings we may live Christ, but do we live Christ at home with our husband or wife and with our children? We need a real revival to be God-men who live a life of always denying ourselves and being crucified to live Christ for the expression of God. (*Life-study of 1 & 2 Chronicles,* pp. 75-77)

Further Reading: Life-study of 1 & 2 Chronicles, msgs. 3, 11; *Life-study of Psalms,* msg. 40; *The Recovery of God's House and God's City,* ch. 7; *Life-study of Ezra,* msgs. 4-5; *Life-study of Nehemiah,* msg. 3

Enlightenment and inspiration: _____

_____

_____

_____

Morning Nourishment

2 Tim.   And the things which you have heard from me
2:2   through many witnesses, these commit to faithful
men, who will be competent to teach others also.

1 Tim.   ...*I write* that you may know how one ought to con-
3:15   duct himself in the house of God, which is the church
of the living God, the pillar and base of the truth.

2 Pet.   Therefore I will be ready always to remind you con-
1:12   cerning these things, even though you know *them*
and have been established in the present truth.

Just as people have different tastes in food, so the Lord's recovery also has a taste for the ministry that has built up the recovery
over the years. The recovery was raised up with a certain taste.
Those who have been raised with this taste will reject a taste that
is contrary to it. This means that if you speak something contrary
to the taste of the Lord's recovery, your speaking will be rejected,
and you will be the first to suffer loss. We have seen a number of
examples of this in the past.

Concerning a matter such as this, it is useless to argue about
who is right and who is wrong. The point here is that saints have a
taste, and they do not accept what is contrary to it. (*Elders' Training, Book 3: The Way to Carry Out the Vision,* pp. 129-130)

Today's Reading

Those who teach differently are not wise, for they do not know
the environment, situation, and condition of the Lord's recovery.
The Lord's recovery has been raised up in a particular way. Brothers who teach differently actually are trying to bring in a foreign
element; they are trying to wedge in a foreign particle into the
"body" of the recovery. The recovery will not accept any kind of foreign element or article. As we have strongly emphasized, the reason is that the saints have their taste.

Although the recovery is not controlled by any person, there is
a controlling factor in the Lord's recovery, and this factor is the
taste in the recovery. The recovery has a particular taste because
it has a certain life that came from its birth.... The Lord's recovery

was born with the life that has its own particular taste. This taste is the controlling factor in the Lord's recovery.

I do not insist that all the churches use the Life-study messages. However, I wish to point out that this ministry brought the recovery to this country and has been helping and nourishing the recovery. The recovery has grown up with the "food" provided by this ministry. Now it is impossible for the saints to change their taste. If you try to change the taste of the saints, you will be foolish, you will waste your time, and you will cause damage. If you feel that your teaching is better than that in the Lord's recovery, you should serve your "food" to those who have a taste for it. Those who have been raised on certain foods may occasionally eat something different. But for the long run in their daily living they will eat what matches their taste and reject what is contrary to it.

Since this is the situation among the saints in the Lord's recovery, we should be wise to learn the basic truths and then serve these truths to the saints. If we do this, everyone will be happy, and we shall have a peaceful situation, not only among individual saints, but also between the churches and between the churches and the ministry.

Whatever we minister must be of the nature of the New Testament ministry. Whether or not a particular ministry is part of the New Testament ministry can be proved by applying three governing principles: one, the principle of the processed Triune God being dispensed into His chosen people; second, the principle of Christ and the church; and third, the principle of Christ, the Spirit, life, and the church. If your teaching can pass this threefold test, your teaching is part of the New Testament ministry. Any ministry that is part of the New Testament ministry will be welcomed by the saints in the Lord's recovery. Any other ministry, however, will only cause trouble for the recovery. (*Elders' Training, Book 3: The Way to Carry Out the Vision,* pp. 130-132)

Further Reading: Elders' Training, Book 3: The Way to Carry Out the Vision, ch. 12

Enlightenment and inspiration: _____

_____

_____

_____

Morning Nourishment

Eph. That by revelation the mystery was made known to
3:3-4 me, as I have written previously in brief, by which, in
reading *it,* you can perceive my understanding in
the mystery of Christ.

9 And to enlighten all *that they may see* what the economy of the mystery is, which throughout the ages
has been hidden in God, who created all things.

2 Tim. For which I was appointed a herald and an apostle
1:11 and a teacher.

3:16 All Scripture is God-breathed and profitable for
teaching, for conviction, for correction, for instruction in righteousness.

In the Summer School of Truth you should present a teaching
that is an unveiling, the rolling away of the veil. Then the young
people in your class will see something of God, and what they see
will rebuke them, correct them, and afford them the proper instruction in righteousness to make them right both with God and
with man. The issue, the outcome, will be that the man of God becomes complete and equipped for every good work.

The purpose of the Summer School of Truth is not to give
mental knowledge to the young people. The goal of our summer
school is to present teaching after teaching, revelation after revelation, so that the young ones may see God, see themselves, and
be reproved, corrected, and instructed to be right with God and
man that the man of God may be complete, fully equipped for
every good work. Such a person will be a true man of God, a
real God-man, continually inhaling the Triune God and thereby
receiving revelation, reproof, correction, and instruction in
righteousness. (*Teachers' Training,* pp. 15-16)

Today's Reading

What is teaching? How do you understand the word *teaching*?
We need to know the denotation of this word as it is used by Paul.

If we have the proper and adequate spiritual experience, we
will realize that in 2 Timothy 3:16 teaching equals revelation.

Teaching is actually nothing less than a divine revelation. Since teaching equals revelation, as you are teaching the young people in your class in the Summer School of Truth, you must present a revelation to them.

A revelation is the opening of a veil. As you are teaching the young people, you should be taking away a veil so that they may see something of the Triune God. A certain matter may be hidden from view, but by your teaching you should gradually open the veil. This is teaching....As they are listening to you, the veil should be rolled away little by little.

Now we can see that for the Bible to be profitable for teaching means that it is profitable for unveiling, for rolling away the veil. A veil cannot be taken away suddenly; it cannot be rolled away all at once. On the contrary, the veil is rolled away a little at a time. Time after time and in session after session, you need gradually to roll away the veil. If you do this, your way of teaching will be an unveiling. This kind of teaching always presents a revelation to others. Those who are under such teaching will be able to see something concerning the Triune God.

This understanding of teaching applies not only to those who teach in the Summer School of Truth but to all those who speak for the Lord. When you speak something in the church meeting, your speaking should be the rolling away of the veil. This means that your speaking should present a revelation.

It is significant that in verse 16 teaching is followed by conviction, or reproof. The reason for this is that no one can see something of God without being reproved by what he sees. Those who are under your teaching will see something, and what they see will convict, reprove, them.

When in our reading of the Scriptures we receive a revelation, the revelation will reprove us and rebuke us. (*Teachers' Training*, pp. 12-13)

Further Reading: Teachers' Training, ch. 1; Life-study of 1 & 2 Kings, msgs. 8, 13; Life-study of Psalms, msg. 16

Enlightenment and inspiration: _____

_____

_____

Morning Nourishment

1 Tim. ...Our Savior God, who desires all men to be saved
2:3-4 and to come to the full knowledge of the truth.
Col. Let the word of Christ dwell in you richly in all
3:16 wisdom, teaching and admonishing one another...
1 Tim. If you lay these things before the brothers, you will
4:6 be a good minister of Christ Jesus, being nourished with the words of the faith and of the good
teaching which you have closely followed.

You need to study the Life-study messages....If you merely read the Life-studies, you will only receive a temporary nourishment. That will only become a kind of inspiration to you. An inspiration is like a vapor in the air....What I have received from the Lord is always the solid truth, so it remains in me, nourishing me all the time. You must have the truth. The only way for the truth to get into you is through your mentality. Then it remains in your memory. If you do not understand, the truth cannot get into you. The truth gets into you through your mentality, your understanding. Also, if the truth gets into your memory, it becomes a constant and long term nourishment. Then you have an accumulation of the truth, and you are a person continually under the constant nourishment. You will then know how to present the truth to others, not merely to inspire them or to stir them up, but to make them solid and constituted with the truth. (*Elders' Training, Book 3: The Way to Carry Out the Vision*, pp. 93-94)

Today's Reading

The biggest shortage [among us today] is that the elders are short of the full knowledge of the truth. I appreciate 1 Timothy in that it deals with the matter of the truth. In John 17:17 the Lord prayed, "Sanctify them in the truth; Your word is truth." The truth, the word, not only regenerates, feeds, and enlightens, but it sanctifies. God desires all men, after being saved, to come to the full knowledge of the truth. No need to say all men, I even doubt all the elders in the recovery have come to the full knowledge of the truth. We should not merely have the knowledge of the truth, but the full knowledge, the complete knowledge, the perfect knowledge, of the truth. In the 1984 elders' training, thirty-six messages were given. I really doubt that you have entered into the full knowledge of those truths which were delivered to you then. If we have never been constituted with this knowledge, then how could we speak? How could we preach? How could we teach?

In Revelation 22 the Lord told us He would come soon (v. 12). Two thousand years have passed, and He has not come yet....The believers [have] delayed Him by ignorance, by not having a full knowledge of the truth. Under the ignorance of all the believers, the Lord just could not find a way to go on. This ignorance is still prevailing today.

Christians today are shallow because they would not pay the price to labor adequately. These riches are all here in the Bible, just like gold in a mine, but nearly no one would labor to dig them out. Just to buy a few pieces of gold is not our job. Our job is to dig the gold mine. We are to do the mining work. This is the Lord's recovery. I hope, brothers, that in your localities you would not repeat the old things. We should learn to go on, to learn the things in the heavenlies, and to learn to speak these higher and deeper things. The book of Revelation, for example, has never been opened up to the Lord's children as it is today. This is now an absolutely transparent book to us. All the points have been covered in the Life-study messages, and the footnotes of the Recovery Version. If you want to know them, you can go to the printed pages and you will get them. This will require your time. To dig out the gold is not that easy. I would encourage all of us to go on in this way....Let us go on. There is real hope for us to go on in His recovery. (*Elders' Training, Book 5: Fellowship concerning the Lord's Up-to-date Move*, pp. 40-41, 51-52, 57-58)

Further Reading: Elders' Training, Book 3: The Way to Carry Out the Vision, ch. 9; Elders' Training, Book 5: Fellowship concerning the Lord's Up-to-date Move, ch. 3; The Subjective Truths in the Holy Scriptures, chs. 1-3; Crystallization-study of Song of Songs, msg. 9

Enlightenment and inspiration: _____

_____

_____

_____

Morning Nourishment

Eph. And for me, that utterance may be given to me in
6:19 the opening of my mouth, to make known in boldness the mystery of the gospel.
1 Cor. Which things also we speak, not in words taught by
2:13 human wisdom but in words taught by the Spirit,
interpreting spiritual things with spiritual *words*.

We have seen that the vision in the Bible which governs and
controls us is the economy of God. We have also seen the crystallized significances of the various steps of God's economy. I hope
the brothers and sisters will be able to see that our expressions
are absolutely different from the traditional expressions used in
Christianity. We have been enlightened by the Lord to have the
new expressions; we must learn all these new expressions and
new utterances. Even when we knock on doors to visit people, we
should begin our speaking with God's economy. Whether one receives it or not, it is up to him; but the speaking is up to us. We
should not speak the same old things which people have already
heard; we need to speak the crystallized significances of God's
economy. Only these things can thoroughly save people; so we
need to learn to speak them. (*The Governing and Controlling
Vision in the Bible*, p. 23)

Today's Reading

In the Lord's recovery we are a special group of people with our
own culture. Since we have this culture, we need the language to
match it. Expressions such as *processed* and *ultimate consummation* have become very common among us, yet they are new both
in the English and Chinese languages. If we have not been weigh-
ing and considering the truth to invent some new terms, how can
we explain our particular culture? This is a spiritual culture, a
heavenly culture, and a culture in God's economy. It can be ex-
plained not with any language on earth but only with the spiritual, heavenly language.

When the Western missionaries began to translate the Bible
into Chinese, they could not translate expressions such as *in Christ*

because in the Chinese culture there are only expressions such as *by, through,* and *because of.* Yet the Bible often uses expressions such as *in grace, in power, in the light,* and *in reality.* For example, the Chinese Union Version renders Philippians 3:1 as, "Rejoice by the Lord," while another version renders it as, "Rejoice because of the Lord," yet the original text says, "Rejoice in the Lord." Noah's family of eight entered into the ark and was saved in the ark, not outwardly by the ark; they could have peace only in the ark. Because of this problem, some Western missionaries created the new expression *in Christ* in Chinese to speak the new culture with new language. Today those who learn computers have their technical terms that are not understandable to outsiders. Every message that we have released in the recent two years is almost all new language, yet our understanding is still not adequate. We need to endeavor to enter into the new spiritual language that we may be able to express the spiritual truths in a crystallized way.

What we have been speaking is the utterance and expression given to us by the Lord. Traditional theologians in Christianity say that we should not create new terms lightly. They say that it was all right for the church fathers to create expressions such as *the Triune God,* but we should not create any more new expressions lest we stir up trouble. This is due to their ignorance of the truth and their deficiency in experience. Language is a product of culture. If a certain thing exists in a certain culture, there is a definite term in that culture to express that thing....In these years since we have seen something of the Lord and have received from the saints who were before us, we have found out that there is the need to have a new vocabulary to express the truths which we have seen. (*The Governing and Controlling Vision in the Bible,* pp. 27-28, 70)

Further Reading: The Governing and Controlling Vision in the Bible, chs. 1-3, 5; How to Be a Co-worker and an Elder and How to Fulfill Their Obligations, chs. 1-4; The Triune God's Revelation and His Move, msg. 12; Crystallization-study of the Gospel of John, msg. 8; The Divine and Mystical Realm, ch. 5

Enlightenment and inspiration: _____

_____

_____

Morning Nourishment

2 Tim. Be diligent to present yourself approved to God, an
2:15 unashamed workman, cutting straight the word of
     the truth.
Neh. And on the second day the heads of fathers' *houses*
8:13 of all the people, the priests, and the Levites were
     gathered to Ezra the scribe, that is, in order to gain
     insight into the words of the law.

Millions of copies of the Bible have been distributed....Nearly everywhere you go today you find a Bible, but who has entered into the Bible? There has nearly been no entrance. Many have a copy of the Bible, but the Bible has been closed and nearly never opened. Now the Lord has given us a key, an opener. I consider our writings as the opener to open the holy Word. I believe that those of you who have read the Life-study messages can testify honestly that these messages with the notes of the Recovery Version have opened up a certain chapter or a certain book of the Bible to you. This is not to replace the Bible, but to bring people into the Bible.

Based upon this, I feel that for the long range for the Lord's recovery in such a top country as the United States, which is full of culture, education, scientific knowledge, and biblical knowledge, the greatest need we must meet is to bring the saints in the Lord's recovery into the truth to carry the Lord's recovery on. (*Elders' Training, Book 3: The Way to Carry Out the Vision*, pp. 103-104)

Today's Reading

The basic truths have been presented to us, and much life nourishment has been put into print, especially with the Life-study messages. Also, the obstacles have nearly all been removed. We now have a clear way for our study, and every book is open to us. In mining, the hardest thing is to open the mine. Once the mine has been opened and the treasure is exposed, it is easy for someone to dig out the treasures. I have left only this one matter of further digging to you....After a period of time I believe that many of you will be "good diggers." The intention and the goal of our publishing of the Life-study messages is to open up the mine for you to go in and dig.

Some condemn us and slander us by saying that we take the Life-study messages more than the Bible and even as the Bible because we use them so much. We must ask, though, which students of the Bible and which teachers of the Bible have never used commentaries, expositions, or other books. Commentaries and expositions are not for the purpose of replacing the Bible but for the purpose of opening up the Bible, which is somewhat hard for us to enter in. Because we need the help of reference books, this does not mean that we replace the Bible with reference books. Those of us who have read the Life-study messages can testify that these Life-study messages with the Recovery Version and all the footnotes open the Bible to us whenever we touch them. The Life-study messages and the Recovery Version not only convey the nourishment to us, but they become an opener.

For years I have been a very devoted seeker of biblical truth. Romans 8 was seemingly opened to me before 1954, but I did not realize that it was still concealed to me.... [In Romans 8] we must see that the processed Triune God is dispensing Himself into His redeemed, tripartite man, making this man a man of life—first his spirit is life (v. 10), then his mind becomes life (v. 6), and finally, life is given to his mortal body (v. 11). Until you have seen such a vision you could never enter into Romans 8. Without such a vision, Romans 8 is concealed and closed to you. Once you have received such a vision, however, you will receive not only nourishment but enlightenment. You receive the key that opens Romans 8. This is not replacing the Bible. This is not replacing Romans 8 with the Life-study messages, but this is to get the help from the Life-study messages to enter into Romans 8. (*Elders' Training, Book 3: The Way to Carry Out the Vision*, pp. 93, 53-54)

Further Reading: Elders' Training, Book 3: The Way to Carry Out the Vision, chs. 1, 3, 5-6, 8-13; The Vision of the Divine Dispensation and Guidelines for the Practice of the New Way, ch. 7; The Full Knowledge of the Word of God, ch. 1

Enlightenment and inspiration: _____

_____

_____

_____

Hymns, #801

1   O living Word of God, God's image true,
       Thou art the content of God's written word;
       God in Thee we have met, God's fulness found,
       And in the Scripture we Thyself have heard.

2   No man has e'er seen God, apart from Thee,
       Without the Scripture Thee we'd hardly see;
       Thou to the human race God hast declared,
       And thru the Scripture Thou art shown to me.

3   Perfect embodiment Thou art of God,
       A portrait full the Scripture gives of Thee;
       In Thee we comprehend God's image true,
       And thru the Scripture Thou art real to me.

4   Life-giving Spirit Thou, as well as Word,
       Now e'en the Spirit in the Word Thou art;
       When thru the Spirit giv'n, I touch the Word,
       Fulness divine to me Thou dost impart.

5   In Thee I may with God have fellowship,
       And thru the Scripture I on Thee may feed;
       Thru study of the Word with prayer to God
       Thy glorious riches fully meet my need.

6   Teach me to exercise my spirit, Lord,
       Thy Word to study, so to contact Thee,
       That Thou, the living Word, with Scripture, too,
       As one my daily manna e'er may be.

Composition for prophecy with main point and sub-points: _____

_____

_____

_____

_____

_____

_____

_____

_____

_____

_____

_____

_____

_____

_____

_____

_____

_____

_____

_____

_____

_____

_____

_____

_____

_____

_____

_____

_____

_____

_____

_____

_____

_____

_____

_____

_____

_____

Reconstitution

Scripture Reading: Neh. 8:1-3, 5-6, 8, 13; Eph. 3:16-17a,
   19b, 21; 4:4-6; Rev. 21:2, 10-11

Day 1 **I. God's intention with Israel was to have on
earth a divinely constituted people to be His
testimony—a people reconstituted with the
word of God (Isa. 49:6; 60:1-3; Col. 3:16):**

A. After the return from captivity, the people of Israel
were still unruly, for they had been born and raised
in Babylon and had become Babylonian in their
constitution:

1. In order for them to be citizens of the nation of
Israel, they needed to be reconstituted (Neh.
8:1-3, 5-6, 8, 13).

2. They needed to be educated with the word
which comes out of the mouth of God and
which expresses God (Psa. 119:2, 9, 105, 130,
140; Col. 3:16).

B. Because Ezra bore the totality of the divine constitution and culture, through him the people could
be reconstituted with the word of God (Neh. 8:1-2):

1. Ezra brought the people back to the Word of
God that they might be re-educated and reconstituted with the truths in the divine Word
(vv. 8, 13).

2. There was the need of reconstitution to bring
the people of God into a culture that was according to God and that expressed God (Col.
3:10-11):

a. In the Lord's recovery we are a special
group of people with our own culture, a
divine and heavenly culture (Rev. 1:4-6;
5:9-10).

b. We need to learn the new language with
the new vocabulary of the new culture of
the Lord's present recovery (1 Cor. 2:12-16;
Neh. 13:23-24).

C. The returned captives were reconstituted person-
ally and corporately to become God's testimony; by
this kind of divine constitution, they became God
in life and in nature—a divine nation expressing
the divine character (1 Pet. 2:9).

II. **God's eternal intention is to work Himself in
Christ into us and to reconstitute us with Himself so that we may become His corporate expression—the Body of Christ, the new man,
consummating in the New Jerusalem (Eph.
3:17a; 4:4, 16, 24; Rev. 21:2):**

A. The entire Bible was written according to the principle of the Triune God working Himself into His
chosen and redeemed people (Psa. 36:8-9):

1. This principle must govern and direct us in
interpreting any portion of the Bible (Prov.
29:18a).

2. We need to be constituted with this principle,
and it must become a vision to us; as a result,
there will be an intrinsic principle within us,
governing whatever we speak, teach, and
preach (Acts 26:19).

Day 2   B. God's central work is to work Himself in Christ
into His chosen and redeemed people to make
them His corporate expression (Eph. 3:16-17a, 19b,
21):

1. We need God to build Christ into our intrinsic
constitution so that our entire being will be reconstituted with Christ (v. 17a).

2. Only those who have been reconstituted with
Christ are qualified to be built up as the
church, God's dwelling place today (vv. 16-17a;
2:21-22).

Day 3   C. God's intention is to change our constitution by
changing our diet and feeding us with Christ (Exo.
16:14-15; John 6:27, 35).

Day 4   D. For the fulfillment of God's economy, we need to
deal with the natural constitution—the expression
of the living out of the old man that is related to

human ability, capability, wisdom, cleverness, schemes, and skills (1 Cor. 2:14; 2 Cor. 1:12; James 3:15; Phil. 3:3-7).

E. God's intention with Job was to reduce him to nothing yet maintain his existence in order to impart Himself into him (Job 1:1, 8; 42:5-6).

F. We need to become a constitution of grace, which is the Triune God processed, consummated, and dispensed into us for our enjoyment (2 Cor. 13:14).

G. The ministry of the new covenant is a constitution of life and in life (4:1, 10).

Day 5

H. The meaning of the new creation is that the Triune God dispenses Himself into us, mingles Himself with us, and constitutes us with Himself to make us new (5:17; Gal. 6:15).

I. In substitution Christ was made sin for us; now in His constitution we become the righteousness of God in Him (2 Cor. 5:21).

J. Christ came as a Physician to heal, recover, enliven, and save us so that we might be reconstituted to be His new and heavenly citizens, with whom He can establish His heavenly kingdom on this corrupted earth (Matt. 9:12-13).

K. The Body of Christ is a divine constitution of the Triune God with the believers in Christ; the essential, crystallized significance of the Body of Christ is that the Triune God is constituted together with His chosen and redeemed people to become a single, constituted entity (Eph. 4:4-6).

L. The divine fellowship reconstitutes us, for this fellowship brings the divine constituent into our spiritual being, causing a change in our being (1 Cor. 1:9; 1 John 1:3).

Day 6

M. The new man is Christ in all the believers permeating us and replacing us until all natural distinctions have been removed and everyone is constituted with Christ (Eph. 4:24; Col. 3:10-11).

N. The distinction of social rank and status among
the believers is nullified by an inward change of
constitution; according to our new constitution,
we are all the same (Gal. 3:27-28; Col. 3:10-11).

O. The New Jerusalem is built by God's constitut-
ing Himself into man to make man the same as
He is in life and nature but not in the Godhead
so that God and man may become a corporate
entity and be a mutual dwelling place (Rev.
21:2-3, 10-11, 18-22):

1. Our unique work is to make God's chosen,
redeemed, and regenerated people beings
in the New Jerusalem (3:12; S. S. 6:4).

2. "The processed and consummated Triune
God, according to the good pleasure of His
desire and for the highest intention in His
economy, is building Himself into His chosen people and His chosen people into Himself, that He may have a constitution in
Christ as a mingling of divinity and humanity to be His organism and the Body of
Christ, as His eternal expression and the
mutual abode for the redeeming God and
the redeemed man. The ultimate consummation of this miraculous structure of treasure will be the New Jerusalem for
eternity" (Witness Lee).

Morning Nourishment

Psa.   **They are saturated with the fatness of Your house,**
36:8-9 **and You cause them to drink of the river of Your**
        pleasures. For with You is the fountain of life; in
        Your light we see light.

2 Tim. **Be diligent to present yourself approved to God, an**
2:15   **unashamed workman, cutting straight the word of**
        the truth.

Acts   **...I was not disobedient to the heavenly vision.**
26:19

Even in the dispensation of law before the dispensation of the New Testament age, the seeking saints were enjoying the Triune God....How much more should we then enjoy the Triune God in such a high way today in His dwelling place on this earth, the church. Where is the church?...The proper church is a house where the fatness of Christ is satisfying people, where the Spirit flows as the river of God's pleasures, and where the fountain of life and light could be found. This is the church,...and this will consummate in the New Jerusalem where the Triune God will be our enjoyment in the same way.

Some of you have been reading, studying, and reciting Psalm 36:8-9 for years, but you could not and did not interpret these verses in this way. The only way we could interpret these verses in this way is by the governing vision—the Triune God is working Himself into His chosen and redeemed people to be their life and life supply, to saturate their entire being with the Divine Trinity, that is, with the Father as the fountain, the Son as the fatness, and the Spirit as the river. This is the vision that governs and directs you to interpret any portion of the Bible. (*Elders' Training, Book 2: The Vision of the Lord's Recovery,* pp. 157-158)

Today's Reading

Any book of the Bible must be interpreted by such a governing vision. Without such a vision, you may present a good message based upon Psalm 36:8-9, yet it will be so shallow, touching nothing of the Divine Trinity....[You may] discover that *the fatness* refers to the fatty ashes of the sacrifices, [but] without such a vision you would never think that this refers to Christ. You must have the governing principle. Then when you see the word sacrifices, you would be so clear that this refers to the second of the Divine Trinity, Christ. Then it would also be easy for you to understand the river of God's pleasures....Romans 14:17 refers back to this river when it tells us that the kingdom of God is "righteousness and peace and joy in the Holy Spirit." The joy in the Holy Spirit is the river of pleasures.

The entire Bible was written according to the principle of the Triune God wrought into His redeemed people as their enjoyment, their drink, and their fountain of life and light. The application of this principle in interpreting any portion of the New Testament is endless. Then your message, using any portion, will be greatly enriched....There will be an intrinsic principle within and governing whatever you speak, teach, and preach. This is my burden. Merely to read the lines of a Life-study to pick up some points and titles for our message does not work. You have not been constituted with such a principle, and this principle has not become a vision to you. You may have the eyes to read the Bible and the mind to understand it, but you do not have the key to open it. You need the key.

A certain message may be wonderful, eloquent, and very inspiring, yet in principle that may be a distracting message, a holding back message. We could be laboring for ten years, but by one message people could be held back for five years. Still, most of the people who listen may appreciate that kind of message. To discern this, you need this basic principle of this vision to see that the Triune God is the very essence and should be the very essence of every message that we put out. Only this serves God's purpose, only this keeps us from being led astray, and only this can keep us in oneness from today through eternity. (*Elders' Training, Book 2: The Vision of the Lord's Recovery*, pp. 158-159, 162)

Further Reading: Elders' Training, Book 2: The Vision of the Lord's Recovery, ch. 13; *Crystallization-study of the Gospel of John*, msg. 2; *Life-study of Ezra*, msg. 5; *Life-study of Nehemiah*, msgs. 4-5

Enlightenment and inspiration: _____

_____

_____

_____

Morning Nourishment

Eph. **That He would grant you, according to the riches of**
3:16-17 **His glory, to be strengthened with power through**
His Spirit into the inner man, that Christ may make
His home in your hearts through faith...
19 **...That you may be filled unto all the fullness of God.**

In 2 Samuel 7 David, like many of us, had the mistaken concept that God needed him to build something for Him. When some hear this they may wonder how this concept can be wrong since we today are endeavoring to build up the church. Is building the church not a matter of building something for God? To answer this question we need to realize that apparently we are the ones who are building the church, but actually God is the One who is building the church with Christ as the unique element. When we are about to do some building work by speaking for God, He may check with us, saying, "Do you intend to build My house? With what material will you build My house?" If we say that we are building up the church with Christ, God may ask us how much we have of Christ. This exposes our shortage of Christ. We need Christ not merely in name and in knowledge; we need the real Christ, Christ as the Spirit in resurrection. We all need more and more of Christ. (*Life-study of 1 & 2 Samuel,* pp. 159-160)

Today's Reading

The church is not built with the knowledge of the Bible. The church is built with Christ as the unique element. Many times, after trying to build up the saints with Christ, I have had to ask myself, "How much of Christ have you really ministered to the saints? Did you minister only doctrine and the high truths concerning God's economy, or did you minister the real Christ, the genuine Christ, the reality of Christ in resurrection as the Spirit?" Then I had to confess my shortage of Christ and repent, saying, "Lord, forgive me. I am still short of You. I need You to be wrought into me. I need more of You to be constituted into my being."

In 2 Samuel 7 David wanted to build God's house, but in this chapter God wanted David to realize that he needed God to build

Christ into him....There is no need for us to build something for God. We simply are not able to do this. We cannot build something for God with ourselves or with our knowledge of the Bible and theology. We need God to build up Christ into our intrinsic constitution so that our entire being will be reconstituted with Christ. As a result, we are not only changed, but we are transformed from one kind of person into another.

At this point we need to consider once again what God's economy is. God's economy is to work Himself into us in Christ as His embodiment. Through death and resurrection Christ has become the life-giving Spirit (1 Cor. 15:45b). Now we need to let God work Christ as the Spirit into every part of our being. The more God does this, the more we will be able to declare, "To me, to live is Christ," and "I am crucified with Christ; and it is no longer I who live, but it is Christ who lives in me" (Phil. 1:21; Gal. 2:20).

The New Testament verse that best indicates that Christ is building Himself into us is Ephesians 3:17. Here Paul says that Christ is making His home in our hearts. This is building. What is of crucial importance today is the question concerning how much of Christ has been built into us. How much has Christ been built not only into your spirit but into your heart in order to make His home there?

Ephesians 3 indicates strongly that the Triune God is building Himself into us in Christ's making us His home. Paul bowed his knees to the Father and prayed that He would grant us, according to the riches of His glory, to be strengthened with power through His Spirit into the inner man (vv. 14, 16) so that Christ may make His home in our hearts. Here we have the Divine Trinity: the Father is the One to whom Paul prayed; the Spirit is the One who carries out the strengthening; and Christ the Son is the One who is making His home in our heart. By building Himself into our being, He makes our heart, our intrinsic constitution, His home. (*Life-study of 1 & 2 Samuel,* pp. 160-162)

Further Reading: Life-study of 1 & 2 Samuel, msgs. 23-31; *The Spirit with Our Spirit,* ch. 12

Enlightenment and inspiration: _____

_____

_____

_____

Morning Nourishment

Exo. ...And Moses said to them, It is the bread which
16:15 Jehovah has given you to eat.
John Work not for the food which perishes, but for the
 6:27 food which abides unto eternal life, which the Son
      of Man will give you...
   35 Jesus said to them, I am the bread of life; he who
      comes to Me shall by no means hunger, and he who
      believes into Me shall by no means ever thirst.

The Lord Jesus is the real manna. In John 6 He indicates that
we should seek Him and eat Him. However, not many Christians
realize the need for a change of diet. All those who have been regenerated need to change their diet. This is the reason that Exodus 16 is even more crucial than Exodus 12. In chapter twelve we
see a people who have been redeemed, but we do not see a people
who have been reconstituted. At the time of chapter fourteen,
God's people had come out of Egypt, but Egypt had not come out of
them. According to their constitution, they were still Egyptians.
Thus, God's intention was to change their constitution by changing their diet. By the time the children of Israel had built the
tabernacle, their diet had been changed. Their constitution had
probably begun to change also. When they were building the
tabernacle, they did not eat Egyptian food. Instead, their diet
consisted of manna. (*Life-study of Exodus*, pp. 410-411)

Today's Reading

The Egyptian diet denotes all the things we desire to feed on in
order to find satisfaction. Such a diet may include television,
sports, music, magazines, newspapers, or other forms of worldly
entertainment. Some people cannot live without television or
newspapers. This indicates that these things are part of their
Egyptian diet. Still others feed on window-shopping. They may
not care to buy anything, but they enjoy looking at things in the
store windows....America is the leading country with respect to
the Egyptian diet. In this country there is a modern Nile River
bearing all manner of worldly supply.

Before we were saved, we all had an Egyptian diet. But after we are saved, we should change our diet. However, many Christians still live according to their old diet after they are saved. This means that they continue to hunger and thirst for the things of the world.

The heavenly diet makes people heavenly. This heavenly diet is actually Christ Himself. He is the food, the manna. Therefore, by eating Christ we become Christ; that is, Christ becomes our very constituent.

The heavenly diet fulfills God's purpose. Those who built the tabernacle were not Egyptians. They were those with a heavenly constitution. It was at least four months after the children of Israel left Egypt that they began to build the tabernacle. During these months, their diet had been changed and their constitution was at least in the process of changing and of being replaced with the element of manna. By feeding on manna, God's people eventually became manna. As those constituted of manna, they could build the tabernacle as God's dwelling place. This picture shows that only those who have been reconstituted with Christ are qualified to build up the church as God's dwelling place today. This is what it means to say that the heavenly diet fulfills God's purpose.

The [Egyptian diet was]...only good to make God's people Egyptian in their constitution....[It] could satisfy their lusts, but...could not enable the people to fulfill God's purpose. In order for God's purpose to be accomplished, His people had to be reconstituted with manna. This reveals that our constitution must be rearranged through the eating of Christ. Christ must replace the Egyptian diet. For the building of the church, we all need to be reconstituted with Christ. Remember that those who built the tabernacle had experienced a change of diet and had begun to be reconstituted with the element of manna. Only such people can build God's dwelling place. In fact, after being reconstituted, they themselves are the dwelling place of God. (*Life-study of Exodus,* pp. 405, 408-409)

Further Reading: Life-study of Exodus, msg. 34; *The Lord's Recovery of Eating,* ch. 1

Enlightenment and inspiration: _____

_____

_____

_____

Morning Nourishment

1 Cor. But a soulish man does not receive the things of
2:14   the Spirit of God, for they are foolishness to him
       and he is not able to know *them* because they are
       discerned spiritually.

Phil. For we are the circumcision, the ones who serve by
3:3   the Spirit of God and boast in Christ Jesus and
       have no confidence in the flesh.

7   But what things were gains to me, these I have
       counted as loss on account of Christ.

Constitution...means "the aggregate of man's physical and mental powers." In the Bible there is no such term as the natural constitution, and it is seldom mentioned among Christians; yet in our experience there is such a thing. It is an outstanding characteristic of the soulish man and a prominent expression of the living out of the old man. If we pursue the experience of the cross, we cannot neglect...dealing with the natural constitution....The natural constitution is the expression of the living out of the old man which has to do with human ability, capability, wisdom, cleverness, schemes, and skills. (*The Experience of Life*, p. 245)

Today's Reading

We have defined the natural constitution as that which pertains to human ability, capability, wisdom, and cleverness, because all these are derived from our natural life and not from the resurrection life of God. They are acquired naturally; they do not spring from resurrection by passing through the breaking in Christ. The difference between the natural constitution and resurrection life is indeed great. Our dealing with the natural constitution is that our inherent ability, capability, wisdom, and cleverness may pass through the death of the cross, become resurrected, and thereby become acceptable and useful to God.

The process of the experience of dealing with the natural constitution closely resembles that of dealing with self....[Seeing that our old man has been crucified with Christ] is the first step toward our experience in dealing with the natural constitution. [Realizing

that the natural constitution is a very strong expression of the old
man] also is a spiritual seeing....This also includes seeing what
the natural constitution refers to and what its expressions are.
After we have seen the first two points, we will automatically
receive the crucifixion of Christ upon our natural constitution.
This also means that we apply the crucifixion of Christ through
the power of the Holy Spirit to our natural expression....It is here
that our natural ability and capability are touched by God, and
the hollow of our thigh, wherein lies the strength of our body, becomes limp. Hereafter, we can no longer as before use our ability
and capability as we wish. Thus, we pass a crisis in our dealing
with the natural constitution; we gain an experience in a subjective way.

In order to apply this experience, we need to apply the death of
the cross through the Holy Spirit....If we live in the fellowship of
the Holy Spirit, we need to let the Holy Spirit execute the crucifixion of Christ upon every area of our natural constitution which we
discover. In other words, every time we discover our cleverness,
wiles, and capability, we must immediately apply the death of the
cross to them. In this way the stamp of the death of the cross is applied to all the practical expressions of the natural constitution.
This is not merely a once for all acceptance; it must also be a daily
application. We must apply the cross to our natural constitution
daily and moment by moment. From the very beginning, when
we accept the working of the cross, we must allow God to touch
every expression of our natural constitution in the fellowship of
the Holy Spirit. We may be rich in thinking and very capable, yet
we must be one that receives the cross and bears the cross; the
cross must continually do the work of breaking us; then after a
certain period of time, all that is of our natural constitution will
gradually be in the state of having passed through death to resurrection. (*The Experience of Life,* pp. 248, 253-254)

*Further Reading: The Experience of Life, ch. 11; Life-study of 2 Corin-
thians, msgs. 37-38; Life-study of Job, msgs. 5, 8-9, 33*

Enlightenment and inspiration: _____

Morning Nourishment

Eph. **One Body and one Spirit, even as also you were**
4:4-6 **called in one hope of your calling; one Lord, one**
faith, one baptism; one God and Father of all, who is
over all and through all and in all.

The Body of Christ is the constitution of the processed Triune God with the transformed human beings. It is constituted by the union of God and man. The Triune God has passed through the processes of incarnation, human living, crucifixion, resurrection, and ascension. The Body of Christ is the constitution of such a processed God with His redeemed people. This constitution has the believers who are redeemed, regenerated, sanctified, renewed, and transformed by God as its outward framework. In other words, the constitution of such a building of God and man has man as its outward framework. However, it is not ordinary men who are the framework, but the believers whom God has redeemed, regenerated, sanctified, renewed, and transformed.

The constitution of the Body of Christ...has also the processed and consummated Triune God as its inward element. Our human body has an outward framework and an inward element. The outward framework plus the inward element are a living and organic body. It is the same with the Body of Christ. The redeemed people are the outward framework; the redeeming God is the inward element. (*The Issue of the Union of the Consummated Spirit of the Triune God and the Regenerated Spirit of the Believers,* pp. 50-51)

Today's Reading

The Father of the Triune God is the source of the inward element of the constitution of the Body of Christ. The Son of the Triune God is the inward element itself. The Spirit of the Triune God is the essence of the inward element. From Ephesians 4:4-6 we can see the source, element, and essence of the Body of Christ. Verse 4 speaks of one Body and one Spirit, verse 5, of one Lord, and verse 6, of one God and Father of all, who is over all and through all and in all. The one Body is the framework; the inward element is the Father as the source, the Son as the element from the Father, and the Spirit as the essence of the element. The Body of Christ is constituted with the Triune God and His redeemed people, with His redeemed people as the outward framework and the Triune God Himself as the inward element.

The building up of the Body of Christ is the growing up of the Body of Christ. Ephesians 4:13 shows us that this growth requires that everyone arrive at a full-grown man, at the measure of the stature of the fullness of Christ. Verse 15 says that we need to grow up into Christ, the Head, in all things. Verse 16 says that the Body will grow gradually unto the building up of itself in love. The growth is the building up.

The building up of the Body of Christ is the issue of the union of the Spirit of God and the spirit of man. It is a constitution in these two spirits. This constitution, this building, has the saved people as its framework and the saving God...as its inward element. All three, the Father, the Son, and the Spirit, are dispensed, transfused, and built into God's redeemed, regenerated, sanctified, renewed, and transformed believers. This dispensing within us is a daily matter. The Triune God—the Father, the Son, and the Spirit—is dispensed and transfused into us day by day and thereby is built into us day by day. This is similar to the foods that we eat. Through digestion, the nutrients of the foods are dispensed into us and transfused into our whole being, and are even built into us to become our element, even to become us. Similarly, the Triune God through His dispensing, transfusing, and building becomes us and is built up together with us. Thus we are growing gradually for the accomplishing of the building up of the Body of Christ. (*The Issue of the Union of the Consummated Spirit of the Triune God and the Regenerated Spirit of the Believers,* pp. 51, 53-54)

Further Reading: The Issue of the Union of the Consummated Spirit of the Triune God and the Regenerated Spirit of the Believers, ch. 4; *The Constitution and the Building Up of the Body of Christ,* ch. 1; *Life-study of Galatians,* msg. 36; *The Triune God to Be Life to the Tripartite Man,* msg. 17; *Life-study of Matthew,* msg. 27

Enlightenment and inspiration: _____

_____

_____

_____

Morning Nourishment

Gal. For as many of you as were baptized into Christ have
3:27-28 put on Christ. There cannot be Jew nor Greek, there
cannot be slave nor free man, there cannot be male
and female; for you are all one in Christ Jesus.

Col. And have put on the new man, which is being renewed
3:10-11 unto full knowledge according to the image of Him
who created him, where there cannot be Greek and
Jew, circumcision and uncircumcision, barbarian,
Scythian, slave, free man, but Christ is all and in all.

In Colossians 4 we have a record of the fellowship of the new
man. Colossians 4:9 speaks of Onesimus, and verse 17, of Archippus, the son of Philemon. A free man and a slave who were members of the same household were also part of the church as the
new man.

The Epistle to Philemon should be regarded as a continuation
of Colossians 4 and considered an illustration of how in the new
man all social rank is put aside....This short Epistle serves the
special purpose of showing us the equality in eternal life and divine love of all the members in the Body of Christ. The distinction
of social rank and status among the believers is nullified not by an
outward legal act, but by an inward change of constitution. Ranks
have been abolished because the believers have been constituted
of Christ's life. Christ's life had been constituted into Philemon,
and the same life with the same divine element had been constituted into his slave, Onesimus. According to the flesh, Philemon
was a master and was free, and Onesimus was a slave and was
not free. But according to the inner constitution, both were the
same. Because of the divine birth and a living by the divine life, all
the believers in Christ have equal status in the church, which is
the new man in Christ, with no discrimination between free and
bond. (*Life-study of Philemon*, pp. 10-11)

Today's Reading

In Colossians 3:10 and 11 Paul speaks of the new man....In

the new man Christ is all the members, and He is in all the members. There is no room for the natural man. There is no room for Americans or Chinese, for British or French, for you or me. In the new man Christ is all. In the church as the new man, Christ is everything. This implies that He is every brother and every sister. This also implies that every brother and sister must be constituted of Christ. In the new man there cannot be Jewish members and Gentile members; there can only be Christ-members. If we would be constituted of Christ, Christ must be added into us more and more. We must be permeated with Christ, saturated with Christ, and have Christ organically wrought into our being. Eventually, we shall be replaced by Christ. Then, in reality, He will be all and in all. He will be every member, every part, of the new man.

The new man does not come into existence by taking Christians from various countries and bringing them together. That would be a new organization, not the new man. The new man comes into being as we are saturated, filled, and permeated with Christ and replaced by Him through an organic process. The new man is Christ in all the saints permeating us and replacing us until all natural distinctions have been eliminated and everyone is constituted of Christ.

Christ as all and in all in the new man should not be mere doctrine. Rather, the rich, substantial Christ must actually be wrought into us organically until He replaces our natural being with Himself. This can take place only as we remain rooted in Him and absorb His riches into us. These riches will then become the substance, the element, which will saturate us organically. Then Christ will become us, and we shall become constituted of Christ. This is not only to grow with Christ, but it is also to be built up in Christ. (*Life-study of Colossians,* pp. 454-455)

Further Reading: Life-study of Philemon, msg. 2; *Life-study of Colossians,* msgs. 30, 35, 39, 44, 52; *Crystallization-study of the Gospel of John,* msg. 16; *The Ten Great Critical "Ones" for the Building Up of the Body of Christ,* msg. 6

Enlightenment and inspiration: _____

_____

_____

_____

Hymns, **#538**

1   It is God's intent and pleasure
     To have Christ revealed in me,
   Nothing outward as religion,
     But His Christ within to be.

    It is God's intent and pleasure
     That His Christ be wrought in me;
    Nothing outwardly performing,
     But His Christ my all to be.

2   It is God's intent and pleasure
     That His Christ may live in me;
   Nothing as an outward practise,
     But Christ working inwardly.

3   It is God's intent and pleasure
     That His Christ be formed in me;
   Not the outward forms to follow,
     But Christ growing inwardly.

4   It is God's intent and pleasure
     That His Christ make home in me;
   Not just outwardly to serve Him,
     But Christ dwelling inwardly.

5   It is God's intent and pleasure
     That His Christ my hope may be;
   It is not objective glory,
     But 'tis Christ subjectively.

6   It is God's intent and pleasure
     That His Christ be all in me;
   Nothing outwardly possessing,
     But His Christ eternally.

Composition for prophecy with main point and sub-points: _____

_____

_____

_____

_____

_____

_____

_____

_____

_____

_____

_____

_____

_____

_____

_____

_____

_____

_____

_____

_____

_____

_____

_____

_____

_____

_____

_____

_____

_____

_____

_____

_____

Separation

Scripture Reading: Neh. 2:4, 10, 17-20; 1 John 2:15-17; 5:4; James 4:4; Rev. 21:18-20; 2:17

Day 1   **I. The intrinsic need in the Lord's recovery is for a remnant of His people to build up the church as the kingdom of God, to "build up the wall," by being fully separated unto God from the world to be fully saturated with God for the church (Neh. 2:4, 10, 17-20; 4:11-23; Rom. 6:19, 22; Eph. 5:26; John 17:17; 2 Pet. 1:4):**

     A. We need to be transformed into precious stones by being constituted with God so that we may be completely separated unto God to be the kingdom of God, the city of God, under the headship of God (Rev. 21:1-2, 10, 18-20; Col. 2:19).

     B. Precious stones indicate transformation; the more we are transformed, the more we are separated and built up together to be one complete wall with its foundations (Rev. 21:12a; 1 Cor. 3:6-12a; Rom. 12:2; 2 Cor. 3:18).

     C. The renewing of the mind and the resulting transformation separate us from our nature that is soaked with the element of the world and save us from a living soaked with the element of the world (Rom. 8:5-6; 12:2, 5-11; Eph. 4:23).

Day 2   **II. The world consists of everything that replaces God and all that usurps man; anything that causes man to disregard God, be removed from Him, or be independent of Him is the world (1 John 2:15-17; James 4:4):**

     A. Satan not only employs the necessities of life, such as people, activities, and things, to preoccupy man, he further organizes them into numerous individual systems to intensify his grip upon man (cf. Gal. 1:4; Eph. 4:14).

     B. The world denotes the enemy's scheme, system, and organization to usurp the place of God in man and to gain full possession of man (cf. Matt. 4:8-11).

C. When man left and lost the presence of God, he invented a godless culture, which will continue to develop until it climaxes in the great Babylon (Gen. 4:16; Rev. 17—18):

1. Satan caused man to employ his entire effort to seek food and clothing for self-nurture, to invent instruments for self-defense, and to design various forms of amusements for self-enjoyment (Gen. 4:16-24).

2. God Himself, the presence of God, is man's provision, protection, and pleasure; when man loses the presence of God, he fears poverty, danger, and boredom with life (cf. Matt. 6:31-33).

Day 3 & Day 4

III. **Babylon as a place of idols, Egypt as a place of worldly riches and pleasures, and Sodom as a city of sin are three aspects of the world that form a triangular boundary around the land of Canaan; God's called ones live within and must be saved from this satanic triangle (Jer. 2:13; 1 John 5:21; 2 Tim. 3:1-5; 2 Cor. 6:14—7:1):**

A. The idolatrous world of Babylon is characterized by the wickedness of business, or commerce, involving covetousness, deceit, and love of money; our Christian life should be without the love of money, and our Christian work should not be a money-making trade (Zech. 5:5-11; 1 Tim. 3:3, 8; 6:5-10; Acts 11:29-30; 20:33-34; 2 Tim. 3:2-4; Heb. 13:5; 2 Cor. 2:17; 12:15; cf. 2 Kings 5:15-27):

1. Satan is a businessman, a merchant, and his thought is according to his commercial principle which is versus God's purpose in creating man (Ezek. 28:16, 18; Job 1:9; cf. Phil. 3:7-8; Gen. 1:26).

2. Of the cargo sold by Babylon, the first item is gold and the last is the souls of men; *souls of men* refers to men who sell themselves for employment (Rev. 18:12-13; cf. 2 Pet. 2:3, 15).

3. This depicts not only the coming Babylon but also today's world; people sell their soul, their life, themselves, to their occupation, neglecting God and their eternal destiny (cf. Luke 12:13-21).

4. God's sovereignty will cause the wickedness in business, which the people of Israel learned from the Babylonians in their captivity, to go back to Babylon (the land of Shinar) (Zech. 5:10-11; Gen. 11:2, 9).

B. Satan uses the world, typified by Egypt with its pleasures and riches, as his anti-God system to keep man under his slavery and bondage (Exo. 1:11):

1. The world is against God's building, and God's building is opposed to the world (John 15:18; 1 John 2:15-17).

2. God's intention in giving His chosen people a revelation of the true nature, meaning, and issue of life in Egypt (the world) is to cause His people to hate and become disgusted with Egypt, to leave Egypt behind, and to be separated to God for His dwelling place (Exo. 5:1; 40:34; Rom. 12:1-2).

3. If we would be God's dwelling place, we must know the world in a thorough way, and the element of the world must be purged out of our being.

4. God desires to rescue His chosen people from every form of usurpation and preoccupation so that they may have nothing besides God Himself (Mark 9:7-8; Psa. 73:25-26; 90:1).

5. God desires that all His people be Nazarites, those who separate themselves unto God to be absolutely, utterly, and ultimately for God, that is, to be for nothing other than God (Num. 6:1-8; Rom. 1:1; 15:16).

Day 5 C. We need to overcome the stupefying effect of the world's indulgent living, signified by the days of Lot, who drifted into the wicked city of Sodom (Luke 17:26-32; Gen. 13:5-13; 14:12; 2 Pet. 2:6-9):

1. In their giving up God, the wicked Sodomites were given up by God to "passions of dishonor"; this is the ultimate issue of man's rebelling against God and rejecting his conscience (Gen. 19:4-16, 30-38; Rom. 1:21-27; 2:14-15; 1 Tim. 4:2).

2. In God's complete salvation, we can be washed from all the sinful things of Sodom, sanctified by God, and justified, accepted, by God; if we glorify God, thank God, worship God, and serve God, we will be protected from every kind of evil (1 Cor. 6:9-11; Rom. 1:21, 25).

3. As Abraham was enjoying sweet fellowship with God, he received a revelation from Him regarding the birth of Isaac and the destruction of Sodom; this signifies that God intends to bring forth Christ in our life and to destroy the "Sodom" in our home life, work life, and even in our Christian and church life (Gen. 18:10, 14, 16-21; Heb. 12:1-4; 1 Cor. 5:7-8; Rom. 8:2).

4. "Remember Lot's wife" is a solemn warning to the world-loving believers (Luke 17:31-32; 19:15-17, 26; 14:34-35; 1 John 2:27-28).

Day 6 IV. **By living in our spirit and eating Christ as the hidden manna, we can overcome the world to become God's building (cf. John 14:30):**

A. As we live in our spirit, we overcome the world, we are kept from sinning, and the evil one cannot touch us; whatever is not in our spirit is an idol (1 John 5:4, 18-19, 21).

B. While the degraded church goes the way of the world, we can come forward to the Holy of Holies to eat the Lord as the hidden manna, the focal point of God's building, for our incorporation into the Triune God (Rev. 2:12-17).

Morning Nourishment

Neh.   ...Come and let us build up the wall of Jerusalem so
2:17   that we will no longer be a reproach.
Rev.   And he...showed me the holy city, Jerusalem, com-
21:10, 12   ing down out of heaven from God....It had a great
       and high wall...
18-19   And the building work of its wall was jasper....The
       foundations of the wall of the city were adorned
       with every precious stone...
2 Cor.   But we all with unveiled face, beholding and reflect-
3:18   ing like a mirror the glory of the Lord, are being
       transformed into the same image from glory to glory,
       even as from the Lord Spirit.

In the church if we are only in the life of Christ, but know nothing of the headship of Christ, there may be breaches in the wall. We may build up the church as the house in the life of Christ, but to have the church as the city, we must realize the headship of Christ. To have a church not only as a house, but as a city for protection, we must go further to take the headship of Christ. Having the life of Christ may be sufficient for the house, but it is not sufficient for the city. The city must be built up with the headship of Christ.

We all need to have our will exercised, renewed, and transformed so that it will be under the headship of Christ. Our will must be subdued to the Head. Then we will be settled. As members of the Body, which is expressed by the local church, we must be willing to be under the headship of Christ. Then we will build up our part of the wall, and there will be no breach.

All the local churches need the building up of the wall. If we have seen the local church as the expression of the Body, then we must see that the Body is under the headship of Christ. We as members are under this headship. There is no choice; we must all be under the authority of Christ. Then the wall will be built. The wall constitutes the city, and the city in typology signifies the kingdom, the government. The Lord is in the house, but the King is in the city for the kingdom. (*The Recovery of God's House and God's City*, pp. 80-81)

Today's Reading

The wall of a city is not only for protection, but also for separation. The wall is a separating line. When the wall is built up, it separates what is within from what is without. In Genesis 2, ...Satan crept in because there was no wall. But at the end of the Bible, there is a...perfect wall to separate what is holy from what is common. Anything that is common has no entrance into the city.

The separation of the wall is not built up with regulations, but with transformed precious stones. The New Jerusalem is a city built up with transformed stones, not pieces of clay. There is not one brick made of clay. The separation of the wall is the building up of the transformed stones. The more we are transformed, the more we are separated, and the transformation eventually becomes the separating line. It is not by regulation, but by transformation. We should not have any regulations in the church concerning how long our hair ought to be or whether our members should shave or not....Our trust is in the growth in life and transformation. Transformation is the separating line. We do not have regulations, but we do have the transforming life. Praise the Lord! This transforming life will bring forth much separation.

In the wall of the New Jerusalem, there is nothing of regulation, but there is the building of the transformed precious stones. If we would pray-read all the verses in Revelation 21 and 22, we would see so much related to life: the flow of life, the feeding on life, the drinking of life, and the transforming of life. This is the church with the wall built up by transformation. (*The Recovery of God's House and God's City,* pp. 81-82)

Further Reading: The Recovery of God's House and God's City, ch. 8; *God's New Testament Economy,* ch. 36; *The Application of the Interpretation of the New Jerusalem to the Seeking Believers,* msg. 3; *Salvation in Life in the Book of Romans,* ch. 3; *To Be Saved in the Life of Christ as Revealed in Romans,* ch. 1

Enlightenment and inspiration: _____

_____

_____

_____

Morning Nourishment

1 John   Do not love the world nor the things in the world....
2:15, 17   And the world is passing away, and its lust, but he who
      does the will of God abides forever.
Matt.   Therefore do not be anxious, saying, What shall we
6:31-33 eat? or, What shall we drink? or, With what shall we be
      clothed? For all these things the Gentiles are anxiously
      seeking. For your heavenly Father knows that you need
      all these things. But seek first His kingdom and His
      righteousness, and all these things will be added to you.

The Bible...divides man's needs into three main categories: provision, protection, and pleasure. In order to maintain his existence, he needs not only the various provisions, such as clothing, food, etc., but also a means of defense to protect himself from being hurt and a form of amusement for his happiness. Therefore, the entire need for human living is included in these three all-embracing categories.

Prior to the fall, God was responsible for providing for these three needs of man. First, before man was created, God had made provision for all necessities of human life. When Adam was in the garden of Eden, various kinds of fruit and vegetables, water, air, sunshine, and a place for shelter were provided.

Second, protection or defense was also God's responsibility in the beginning. Today, man needs self-protection and self-defense, but in the beginning God Himself was his defense and protection. When man is under God's care, he can escape any attack or danger.

Third, pleasure was also God's responsibility. Some people think that amusement is sinful, but this concept is wrong. Happiness is essential to human life and is found in amusement. "And out of the ground Jehovah God caused to grow every tree that is pleasant to the sight and good for food" (Gen. 2:9). All the trees in the garden of Eden not only bore fruit for food, but were also pleasing and enjoyable to the eye, making one happy. God not only prepared this happy environment; at the same time He Himself was the joy of man. If man has God as his enjoyment, then man's joy is fulfilled. (*The Experience of Life*, pp. 70-71)

Today's Reading

In the beginning these three great needs—supply, defense, and amusement—were planned and prepared for by God, even as the needs of children today are planned and prepared for by their parents....Adam in the garden of Eden had no need to worry, plan, or prepare anything for himself, for God was responsible for everything. Since God supplied all man's needs, then in reality God was his life and his all.

Alas, man fell by committing sin and was expelled from the garden of Eden! His relationship with God became abnormal. But God prepared a covering of skins for man's redemption, enabling him to remain in His presence. As yet, man had not lost God. However, during Cain's lifetime man fell deeper into sin. Cain said to God, "You have driven me out this day from the face of the ground, and from Your face I will be hidden" (Gen. 4:14). "And Cain went forth from the presence of Jehovah" (v. 16). Thus man left God's presence completely and lost God.

When he lost God, man naturally lost God's provision, protection, and pleasure. When man lost God's care for his livelihood, he first experienced fear; he feared the lack of supply, defense, and happiness....Therefore, in order to meet the necessities of life and survive, man used his own strength and devised means of supply, defense, and amusement. From this time, man created a godless civilization, [which the Bible calls the world].

Originally, man belonged to God, lived by God and relied entirely upon Him. Now Satan has systematized the world to replace God in providing for man's need. Man, having forsaken God, relied upon the world and was overcome by the world. Therefore, the world consists of everything that replaces God and all that usurps man....Anything that causes man to disregard God, be removed from Him, or be independent of Him is the world. (*The Experience of Life*, pp. 71-73)

Further Reading: The Experience of Life, ch. 5; The Heavenly Vision, ch. 5

Enlightenment and inspiration: _____

_____

_____

_____

Morning Nourishment

Luke 12:21   So is he who stores up treasure for himself and is not rich toward God.

2 Tim. 3:2, 4   For men will be lovers of self, lovers of money, boasters, arrogant, revilers, disobedient to parents, unthankful, unholy,...traitors, reckless, blinded with pride, lovers of pleasure rather than lovers of God.

1 John 5:21   Little children, guard yourselves from idols.

Ur of Chaldea was a place of idols, Egypt was a place of worldly riches and pleasures, and Sodom was a city of sin. These three places form a triangular boundary around the land of Canaan. We, God's called ones, live within this triangle and must be careful lest we fall back to the city of idols, go down to the place of worldly pleasures, or drift into the city of sin. Although Lot stayed away from the land of idols and the place of worldly pleasures, he drifted, like a piece of driftwood, into the city of sin. (*Life-study of Genesis*, p. 694)

Today's Reading

To share in the building of God we must be separated from Babel, the city of idols; we must be kept from Sodom, the city of sin; and we must be delivered out of the two Egyptian cities of treasure and enjoyment. Then we will be in a liberated position, completely available to share in God's building. We must have nothing to do with idols, with sin, or with worldly enjoyment.

Look at the situation of Christianity today: so many are still in Babel, others are in Sodom, and a great number of dear Christians are enslaved in the treasure cities. They are under forced labor, toiling for the building of those cities, for enjoyment and security. There are not many, sorry to say, who are for God's building today. We have traveled quite extensively in this country, yet we have seen few Christians who are really out of Egypt. There are some who have come out of Babel and Sodom, but so many are still entangled by the treasures of this world, by the lust for security and enjoyment. It is difficult to find many Christians who are standing in the position of freedom and availability for God's building. Some indeed know the teaching concerning the exercise of the human spirit to contact Christ as life; yet they are still in the treasure cities. In that position they can surely contact the treasure of worldly enjoyment, but they must give up these cities if they would contact Christ. This is exactly why so many Christians today have such a problem exercising their spirit to contact Christ. So many messages on this subject have very little effect on certain people, because they are still in the treasure cities, they are still entangled in Egypt. They are quick to say, "Look, I'm not in Babel. I have nothing to do with idols. I'm not in Sodom either. I have nothing to do with sin." But can we say that we are not in Egypt, that we are not entangled by the world of security and enjoyment?

Peter, in Acts 3:6, could say, "Silver and gold I do not possess, but what I have, this I give to you." What Peter had was the mighty name of Jesus. Not many Christians could say this today. Yes, they will confess the Lord's name, but the power of that name for them has been lost. They cannot say, "Silver and gold have I none." They can afford a considerable amount of silver and gold. If we would share in the building of God, we must be delivered out of all these cities. If we would exercise our spirit to contact Christ, we must be disentangled from the enjoyment of the world; otherwise, our spiritual exercise will be of no avail.

We must always be on the alert, for we are endangered by these three fronts: Babel, Sodom, and the cities of Egypt. When we are delivered from these, our hands are free for God's building. When we are delivered, Christ is so dear and precious to us. It is then that we know how to exercise our spirit to contact Christ. We can never enjoy Christ as our manna if we are still in Egypt. We can never enjoy Christ as the living water, continuously flowing to quench our thirst, if we are still in Egypt. When we are separated from these cities, we are in a position to share in the building of God. (*The Vision of God's Building*, pp. 43-45)

Further Reading: Life-study of Genesis, msg. 52; The Vision of God's Building, ch. 3; Life-study of Zechariah, msg. 6

Enlightenment and inspiration: _____
_____
_____
_____

Morning Nourishment

Exo. So they set taskmasters over them to afflict them
1:11 with their burdens. And they built storage cities for
Pharaoh, Pithom and Raamses.

Rom. I exhort you therefore, brothers, through the com-
12:1-2 passions of God to present your bodies a living sacrifice, holy, well pleasing to God, *which is* your reasonable service. And do not be fashioned according
to this age, but be transformed by the renewing of
the mind that you may prove what the will of God is,
that which is good and well pleasing and perfect.

God wants His people to see the world for what it is. If the element of the world remains in us, we shall be damaged in relation
to the fulfilling of God's purpose. When the children of Israel
were in the wilderness, they remembered the enjoyment they
had in Egypt. They recalled the taste of the leeks, the onions, and
the garlic (Num. 11:5). Due to this remembrance they had a
problem with God's dwelling place. The same is true of Christians today. Because many Christians are still in Egypt, they can
have nothing to do with God's dwelling place. Even those who
have been separated from Egypt may still remember the pleasure of Egypt. Hence, we all need to see a clear picture of the life
and living in Egypt. (*Life-study of Exodus*, p. 194)

Today's Reading

The world also needs to be unveiled to God's people today.
God wants His people to be His dwelling place on earth. However, this desire can be fulfilled only if we have been delivered
from the world and have nothing besides God Himself....If we
want to see the churches built up in a practical way, we must
come fully out of the world.

On the negative side, the book of Exodus unveils the world.
On the positive side, it reveals God's dwelling place. Firstly, the
true nature, meaning, and issue of life in Egypt are exposed to
God's people. God's intention in giving this revelation is to cause
His people to become disgusted with Egypt, to leave Egypt

behind, and to be separated to God for His dwelling place. The principle is the same today. If we have not been separated from the world, we cannot become God's dwelling place. For the building up of His dwelling place, we must see the world as it really is. Furthermore, we must loathe the world's way of living and be willing to forsake it.

If we see God's purpose as it is disclosed in the book of Exodus, it will be easier for us to understand the significance of the plagues. God's intention in sending the plagues was not only to punish the Egyptians; it was also to expose the Egyptian living. Like the Egyptians in the book of Exodus, the people in the world today have no understanding of the actual situation of life in the world. The worldly people have all been drugged. Under the influence of Satan's drugging, they are happy with their life in the world. They have no realization of what it is to live without God in the world. In their experience, the water of the world needs to be turned into blood. Then they will know the nature of life in the world and the result of living in the world. The nature of life in the world is death, and the result of living in the world is also death.

We need to be deeply impressed with the fact that even the remains of sinful things must be judged. In the eyes of God nothing of Egypt is good. Everything related to Egyptian living, to the living of the world, must be exposed and judged thoroughly. May God expose to us every aspect of the living of the world.

The world is against God's building, and God's building is opposed to the world. God's chosen people are the crucial factor between these two opposing forces. If God's people remain in the world, God cannot do anything. But if they are willing to be rescued from the world unto God, God can work out His purpose on the earth to have His dwelling place. Therefore, God must come in to deal with the usurping world and to educate His people to realize what the world is, so that they may give up the world and remain there no longer. (*Life-study of Exodus*, pp. 195, 211-212)

Further Reading: Life-study of Exodus, msgs. 17-18

Enlightenment and inspiration: _____

_____

_____

_____

Morning Nourishment

Luke   Remember Lot's wife. Whoever seeks to preserve his
17:32-33   soul-life will lose it, and whoever loses it will preserve it alive.
1 John   And now, little children, abide in Him, so that if He is
2:28   manifested, we may have boldness and not be put to
shame from Him at His coming.

Lot's wife was saved from destruction, but she became a pillar of
salt (Gen. 19:15-17, 26; Luke 17:32). In the form of powder, salt is
useful. But when salt becomes a block, it is useless. That Lot's wife
became a pillar of salt meant that she had lost her usefulness in the
hand of God and had become a sign of shame. Today Christianity
helps people only to take care of the matter of salvation or perdition. But the Bible reveals that besides the matter of salvation or
perdition, there is the matter of glory or shame. Lot's wife was not
lost; she was saved from destruction. Eventually, however, she became a shame. Hence, the Lord said in Luke 17:32, "Remember
Lot's wife," warning us that, though we are saved, at the Lord's
coming back we might possibly suffer shame like Lot's wife. Although we are saved, we may become ashamed at the Lord's coming back (1 John 2:28). (*Life-study of Genesis*, pp. 697-698)

Today's Reading

In Luke 17:28-33 the Lord warns us not to look back. Why did
Lot's wife look back? Because some of her children, especially her
daughters, were still in Sodom and because her house and her
clothing also were there. If you read Genesis 19 carefully, you will
see that she was behind Lot. As a couple, they should have gone together; she should not have been behind her husband. But...she...
became a pillar of salt. She looked back to the place where she
loved to live and became a sign of shame for our warning....We see
from [this] that in addition to the matter of salvation, there is the
matter of shame. When the day of judgment arrives, will you share
in the glory or in the shame? We shall not suffer perdition, for our
salvation is assured. However, as this warning example indicates,
we may be put to shame.

Believers who live in the world as the worldly people and seek to save their soul, their soul-life, will suffer shame, as did Lot's wife, and will lose their soul at the Lord's coming back (Luke 17:28-33). Most Christians are like this. Although they are believers, yet they live like worldly people, shopping and dressing in the same way as the worldly people do. Since they live and walk the same as the worldlings, there is no difference between them and the worldly people.

As Abraham was enjoying such sweet fellowship with God, he received revelation from Him regarding the birth of Isaac and the destruction of Sodom. These are the two basic things concerning which God will always deal with us. The birth of Isaac is related to Christ, and the destruction of Sodom is related to God's judgment upon sin. Isaac must come and Sodom must go. This means that Christ must come in and sin must go out....The principle is the same in every aspect of our lives: in our married life, home life, personal life, Christian life, and church life. God's concern is to bring Christ forth through us and to eliminate all the sinful things. He intends to produce Christ and to destroy the "Sodom" in our home life, work life, and even in our Christian and church life. All the revelation that we have received and shall receive from God mostly concerns these two items....Positively we see more of Christ and say, "I have seen something new of Christ. How I hate that I have not lived more by Him." This is the revelation regarding the birth of Isaac, the revelation that Christ will be brought forth in your life. But negatively we see our sins and say, "O Lord, forgive me. There is still so much selfishness, hatred, and jealousy in me. I have so many failures, shortcomings, and even sinful things. Lord, I judge these things and want them destroyed." This, in principle, is God's judgment upon and destruction of sin. In our Christian life, Christ must be brought in and "Sodom" must be destroyed. Likewise, in the church life, Christ must increase and sin must be abolished. (*Life-study of Genesis*, pp. 698, 707-708, 673-674)

Further Reading: Life-study of Genesis, msgs. 52-53

Enlightenment and inspiration: _____

_____

_____

_____

Morning Nourishment

1 John 5:4   For everything that has been begotten of God overcomes the world; and this is the victory which has overcome the world—our faith.

18-19   We know that everyone who is begotten of God does not sin, but he who has been begotten of God keeps himself, and the evil one does not touch him. We know that we are of God, and the whole world lies in the evil one.

21   Little children, guard yourselves from idols.

I hope we would all realize that there is something in us that has been begotten of God—our spirit. We may be in the worst place in the world, but our spirit will still say, "Get out of here! Stop fooling around here! How meaningless this is!" We may say that this is the Lord Jesus speaking to us. However, where is He when He speaks to us? He speaks to us not in our mind or in our emotions but in our regenerated spirit. "Everything that has been begotten of God overcomes the world" [1 John 5:4].

Furthermore, 1 John 5:18 says, "He who has been begotten of God keeps himself." As regenerated believers we have been begotten of God specifically in our spirit. Thus, our regenerated spirit, as that which has been begotten of God, keeps us from sinning. We all can testify that many times we have been kept by this spirit which has been begotten of God....Perhaps while you were on your way to a movie theater, something within you said, "Go home! What are you coming here for?" After you entered the theater, something within said again, "Go home!" Eventually, you had to say, "Forget about this!" Thus, you went home. Who kept you? Who brought you back home? It was the regenerated spirit within you that kept you. We are all vile sinners and are all capable of committing gross sins, yet all these years we have been kept. This is because our regenerated spirit has kept us. Within us we have something that has been regenerated, something that has been begotten of God. This something is our spirit. (*Living in the Spirit,* pp. 59-60)

Today's Reading

Finally, there is a warning: "Little children, guard yourselves from idols" (1 John 5:21). This means that anything that is not of the true God, not of the eternal life, and not in the regenerated spirit is an idol. Our reading of the Bible may be an idol, our prayer may be an idol, and even our bread-breaking may be an idol, because we may be reading the Word, praying, worshipping, serving, and even breaking bread outside of our regenerated spirit! We may be lying in the evil one because we are not in the spirit.

You may say that there are no idols in your meeting hall. However, you may not realize that your idols are yourselves, your scheming, and your domineering. You may not realize that your desire to win others over so that they will agree with you is an idol. You may not realize that your idol is your insistence on teaching others the spiritual experience you had three years ago. You may love your Bible and insist that others read it the same way you do. This is also an idol. Whatever is not in the spirit is an idol. Whatever is not of the spirit is an idol. If the elders and co-workers in a local church have opinions, they have idols. If we are in the spirit, we will not have any opinions. The Lord Jesus is one, and He is also one in our spirit, so there cannot be any opinion if we are in our spirit. Any church in which there is dissension between the elders and the deacons, among the elders themselves, or between the elders and the co-workers has idols.

What are idols? Whatever is not the true God is an idol. Today the true God is in our regenerated spirit. We abide in Him, and He also abides in us. This is the true God and the eternal life.

For many years I did not understand why this word suddenly appeared at the end of 1 John....One day, however, the Lord showed me this mystery, and then I realized that anything we do that is not in the regenerated spirit and that does not live out the Lord Spirit is an idol. Today there is only one true God, and this true God is in only one place, that is, our spirit. Everything outside of this spirit is an idol. (*Living in the Spirit*, pp. 63-65)

Further Reading: Living in the Spirit, ch. 5; The Issue of Christ Being Glorified by the Father with the Divine Glory, ch. 4

Enlightenment and inspiration: _____

_____

_____

_____

Hymns, #438

1   I've turned my back upon the world
     With all its idle pleasures,
  And set my heart on better things,
     On higher, holier treasures;
  No more its glitter and its glare,
     And vanity shall blind me;
  I've crossed the separating line,
     And left the world behind me.

     Far, far behind me!
     Far, far behind me!
     I've crossed the separating line,
     And left the world behind me.

2   I've left the old sad life of sin,
     Its follies all forsaken;
  My standing place is now in Christ,
     His holy vows I've taken;
  Beneath the standard of the cross
     The world henceforth shall find me;
  I've passed in Christ from death to life,
     And left the world behind me.

     Far, far behind me!
     Far, far behind me!
     I've passed in Christ from death to life,
     And left the world behind me.

3   My soul shall ne'er return again
     Back to its former station
  For here alone is perfect peace,
     And rest from condemnation;
  I've made exchange of masters now,
     The vows of glory bind me,
  And once for all I've left the world,
     Yes, left the world behind me.

     Far, far behind me!
     Far, far behind me!
     And once for all I've left the world,
     Yes, left the world behind me.

4   My choice is made forevermore,
     I want no other Savior;
  I ask no purer happiness
     Than His sweet love and favor;

My heart is fixed on Jesus Christ,
No more the world shall blind me;
I've crossed the Red Sea of His death,
And left the world behind me.

Far, far behind me!
Far, far behind me!
I've crossed the Red Sea of His death,
And left the world behind me.

Composition for prophecy with main point and sub-points: _____

_____
_____
_____
_____
_____
_____
_____
_____
_____
_____
_____
_____
_____
_____
_____
_____
_____
_____
_____
_____
_____
_____
_____
_____
_____
_____
_____
_____
_____
_____
_____
_____

Protection

Scripture Reading: Neh. 2:4, 10, 17-20; 4:17; Zech. 2:5, 8; Titus 1:9; Acts 20:26-35

Day 1 **I. The intrinsic need in the Lord's recovery is for a remnant of His people to build up the church as the kingdom of God, to "build up the wall," for the protection of the church as the house of God (Neh. 2:4, 10, 17-20):**

A. The wall constitutes the city, and the city in typology signifies the heavenly kingdom, the divine government (Rev. 22:1, 3; Rom. 14:17; Isa. 9:6-7).

B. We must build up the wall to protect the church from the idolatry and division of Babylon (1 John 5:21; Jude 19), the worldly pleasures and ways of Egypt (2 Tim. 3:1-5), and the sin and wickedness of Sodom (1 Cor. 6:9-11, 18-20).

C. We must build up the wall to protect the church from the destruction of the destroyers of God's building:

1. The church needs protection from the destruction of those who blow the wind of divisive teachings by stressing things other than the central teaching concerning God's economy (Eph. 4:14; 1 Tim. 1:4).

2. The church needs protection from the destruction of those who preach and teach heresies (2 Pet. 2:1; 2 John 7-11).

3. The church needs protection from the destruction of those who are factious, sectarian, and from those who make divisions (Titus 3:10; Rom. 16:17).

4. The church needs protection from the destruction of those who are ambitious for position (3 John 9).

5. The church needs protection from the destruction of those who are wolves, who do

not spare the flock, and from those who speak perverted things to draw away disciples after themselves (Acts 20:29-30).

II. **We must build up the wall to protect the church by holding to the faithful word, which is according to the teaching of the apostles, the healthy teaching of God's economy (Titus 1:9; Acts 2:42; 1 Tim. 1:3-4; Prov. 29:18a):**

A. We must shepherd the flock of God by declaring to them all the counsel of God, all of God's economy; under the Lord's shepherding, all the evil persons who disturb God's people are kept away from them so that they can dwell in peace and safety to be mingled with God and bound together in oneness (Acts 20:26-35; Ezek. 33:1-11; 34:25; cf. Zech. 2:8; 11:7).

B. By putting out the pure truth from the Word, we can protect the interests of the riches of God's divinity on the earth and the attainments of Christ's consummation (cf. John 17:17; 1 Tim. 3:15).

Day 2 III. **We must build up the wall to protect the church by helping all the saints realize the headship of Christ (Neh. 4:11-23; cf. Ezek. 22:30; Eph. 1:22-23):**

A. We must have our will subdued by Christ and transformed with Christ through sufferings so that it is submitted to the headship of Christ to be rich in the defending power of Christ in resurrection (S. S. 4:1, 4; 7:4a, 5; 2 Cor. 2:14).

B. The building up of the wall is a matter of spiritual warfare, which does not involve our emotion but our will; everyone must keep his position for the building up of the wall and must learn how to build with one hand and fight with the other (Neh. 4:17; cf. Rom. 12:3).

Day 3 C. We must be today's Nazarites, who are separated unto God from all rebellion and live under the headship of Christ (Num. 6:2, 5; Col. 1:18).

Day 4 IV. We must build up the wall to protect the church by fighting the battle in the Body (Rom. 16:20):

A. The Body puts on the whole armor of God and renders protection to every member; we must seek the counsel and covering of the Body to receive the Body's protection and safeguard (Eph. 6:10-20; Matt. 16:18; Acts 21:4, 11-12).

B. Spiritual warfare is in this principle—one will chase a thousand and two will put ten thousand to flight (Deut. 32:30; Eccl. 4:9-12; Exo. 17:11-13).

Day 5 V. We must build up the wall to protect the church by persevering in prayer to be kept from the evil one and to slay the adversary (Matt. 6:13; 26:41; Col. 4:2; John 17:15; 2 Thes. 3:3; Eph. 6:17-18):

A. All of our prayer should be aimed at the interests of God—Christ, the kingdom of God, and the house of God—as the goal in God's eternal economy (1 Kings 8:48; Dan. 6:10).

B. We need to be watchmen on the walls of Jerusalem, men who detest and resist the wearing out tactics of Satan and pray persistently for the accomplishment of God's will (Isa. 62:6-7; Dan. 7:25; 10:11-13, 20; Matt. 6:9-10).

VI. We must build up the wall to protect the church through the overcoming blood of the Lamb, applied to us through our repenting, confessing our sins, and asking God for His purging (Rev. 12:11; Psa. 51:18; cf. Lev. 10:17).

Day 6 VII. We must build up the wall to protect the church by putting on Christ as the weapons of light; the guiding light of the Spirit and the Word becomes our protecting light (Rom. 13:11-14; Exo. 13:21-22; 14:19-20).

VIII. We must build up the wall to protect the church by retreating into our spirit, the secret place of the Most High, the place where we

can hide in the hiding place of God's presence and in the crucified Christ, where we
can overcome the world, where the evil one
cannot touch us, where we cannot sin, and
where we are guarded from idols (Psa. 91:1;
31:20; 43:2a; S. S. 2:14; 1 John 3:9; 5:4, 18, 21).

IX. We must build up the wall to protect the
church by running into the strong tower of
the Lord's name for our safety and salvation
(Prov. 18:10; Zech. 10:12; 14:9; 1 Cor. 12:3b;
Rom. 10:13; Col. 3:17; cf. Isa. 60:18).

X. We must build up the wall to protect the
church by reigning in life:

A. We need to be those who positively and actively
exercise authority for God to rule over all the
confused and lawless situations and destroy the
antagonistic works of the enemy with a reigning
spirit (Rom. 5:17; 2 Tim. 1:6-7).

B. All spiritual work is a form of spiritual warfare;
we who serve the Lord today must live in the position of ascension, working with one hand and
fighting with the other (Neh. 4:17; 1 Tim. 1:18;
2 Tim. 2:3-4; 4:7; cf. S. S. 4:8; 6:10).

XI. We must build up the wall to protect the
church by Christ as our glory:

A. Christ is the glory in the center of the church,
shining through the church to be its protection
of fire (Zech. 2:5; Rev. 21:18, 23; 22:1, 5).

B. God's glory, God's expression, is our protection
(Phil. 1:20; cf. Lev. 7:8).

Morning Nourishment

Neh. 2:17 ...Come and let us build up the wall of Jerusalem so that we will no longer be a reproach.

Rom. 14:17 For the kingdom of God is not eating and drinking, but righteousness and peace and joy in the Holy Spirit.

Rev. 22:3 ...And the throne of God and of the Lamb will be in it...

After recovering the building of the temple, there is still the need to build up the city. Without the city, there is no protection for the temple. The temple is complete; it is the place of the Lord's presence, where we meet and serve the Lord; but it needs protection. The wall of the city is the defense to the temple. Without the wall of the city, there is no protection.

This is a type which we must apply in the New Testament. In the New Testament, the building of the church is first mentioned in the Gospels. After Peter declared that Christ was the Son of God, he was told that the church would be built. The church comes after the knowing of Christ; after we experience Christ, the church comes into existence. At the same time the Lord told Peter that He would give him the keys of the kingdom. Therefore, the kingdom follows the church. These three things are necessary: Christ as the rock, the church, and the kingdom. Christ must be experienced, the church must be built up, and then the kingdom will be brought in. (*The Recovery of God's House and God's City,* p. 75)

Today's Reading

In many of the local churches, there is the real enjoyment of life in the house, but as far as the city is concerned, there are still some breaches in the wall. They still do not have the safeguard. This is why after Zerubbabel, Joshua, and Ezra, there is the need of Nehemiah for the building up of the wall of the city. The enemy hates this even more than the building of the temple. The adversaries did try to hinder, frustrate, and damage the building of the house, but not nearly as much as they opposed with their subtle wiles the building of the city. The enemy knows that the building of the house can be destroyed, but once the building of the city is completed, there is the safeguard of the wall as a defense to protect the house. So what we need for the long run is the building up of the wall. The wall is part of the city which is the safeguard to the house. All the local churches need the building up of the wall. If we have seen the local church as the expression of the Body, then we must see that the Body is under the headship of Christ. We as members are under this headship,...under the authority of Christ. Then the wall will be built. The wall constitutes the city, and the city in typology signifies the kingdom, the government. The Lord is in the house, but the King is in the city for the kingdom. (*The Recovery of God's House and God's City*, pp. 79, 81)

Many are stirred up by the enemy and try their best to destroy the building of the church....The first kind of destroyers are those who blow the wind of divisive teachings by stressing things other than the central teaching concerning God's economy [Eph. 4:14; 1 Tim. 1:4]. For example, the New Testament teaching regarding baptism by immersion is a minor teaching, but the Southern Baptists make it a major teaching and in so doing their teaching becomes divisive. The principle is the same with every denomination: they are built upon a particular teaching, and they teach things other than the central teaching concerning God's economy. Regarding such a situation, Paul exhorted Timothy to remain in Ephesus in order that he might "charge certain ones not to teach different things...rather than God's economy, which is in faith" (1 Tim. 1:3-4). We all need to be careful not to take any teaching, even a scriptural one, and make it a central teaching. Throughout the years Brother Nee and I have not stressed anything other than the central line of God's economy concerning the church for the producing of the Body to consummate the New Jerusalem. This central teaching is not divisive; on the contrary, it builds up the Body. (*The Secret of God's Organic Salvation: "The Spirit Himself with Our Spirit,"* pp. 61-62)

Further Reading: The Recovery of God's House and God's City, chs. 7-8; *The Secret of God's Organic Salvation: "The Spirit Himself with Our Spirit,"* ch. 4; *The Application of the Interpretation of the New Jerusalem to the Seeking Believers,* msg. 3

Enlightenment and inspiration: _____

_____

_____

Morning Nourishment

S. S. Oh, you are beautiful, my love! Oh, you are beauti-
4:1 ful! Your eyes are *like* doves behind your veil; your
hair is like a flock of goats that repose on Mount
Gilead.

4 Your neck is like the tower of David, built for an
armory: a thousand bucklers hang on it, all the
shields of the mighty men.

7:4 Your neck is like a tower of ivory; your eyes, *like*
the pools in Heshbon by the gate of Bath-rabbim;
your nose is like the tower of Lebanon, which faces
Damascus.

[In Song of Songs 4:4] the Lord likens [the seeker's] neck to
the tower of David. We have seen that the hair signifies our will,
and we know that our neck also signifies our will. Those who are
rebellious toward God in the Bible are called stiff-necked (Exo.
32:9; Acts 7:51). So we see that a flock of goats appearing on the
mountain shows the subduing of her will, and the tower of David
illustrates how strong her will is in resurrection. First of all our
will must be subdued; then it must be strong in resurrection.
The natural will must be dealt with, and then we will have a resurrected will. The crucified and subdued will is just like a flock of
goats standing on a mountainside, but the resurrected will must
be like the tower of David builded up as an armory. An armory is
a place where weapons for fighting are kept. (*Life and Building
as Portrayed in the Song of Songs,* p. 67)

Today's Reading

How poetic the Song of Songs is! First, our will must be subdued; then it will be resurrected like the tower of David, the
armory for the spiritual warfare. All the weapons for spiritual
warfare are kept in our subdued and resurrected will. If our
will has never been subdued by the Lord, it can never be a
strong armory to keep all the weapons for the spiritual warfare. All the weapons are mostly defensive, not offensive. It is
not so much a matter of going out to fight as it is a matter of

standing to resist. Bucklers and shields are all for protection in order to stand. In the spiritual warfare, we are not so much on the offensive as we are on the defensive, standing against all the devilish, subtle attacks of the enemy. Most of the items of the armor mentioned in Ephesians 6 are also defensive. There is really no need for us to fight; the Lord has won the battle already.

We simply need to stand and resist all of the enemy's attacks. The bucklers and the shields which protect us against the arrows of the enemy are kept in this tower, which is the subdued and resurrected will of the Lord's seeking one. This is the real maturity in life.

An unsubdued will is, on the one hand, stubborn, and on the other hand, weak. When the enemy comes, the stubborn, unsubdued will always makes an unconditional surrender. We all know this by our own experience. This is especially true with the sisters. The sisters who are stubborn in the matter of submission are the first to surrender when the enemy attacks. But if we have a submissive will, a will that has been subdued like a flock of goats on a mountain side, our will is expressed like a tower of David. When the enemy comes, our will is like the tower of David that holds all kinds of weapons against his attacks.

The secret of the maturity of the seeking one in chapter three is that her will has been completely subdued and resurrected. Of all eight figures, the first one is strongest in the will, and the last one has no will of its own at all. The horse has an exceedingly strong will, but the palanquin and the crown have no will at all. She has come out of her natural will and is now standing in her resurrected will against the enemy. She is like the tower of David builded as an armory for the spiritual warfare. (*Life and Building as Portrayed in the Song of Songs*, pp. 67-68)

Further Reading: Life and Building as Portrayed in the Song of Songs, ch. 6

Enlightenment and inspiration: _____

_____

_____

_____

Morning Nourishment

Num. ...When a man or a woman makes a special vow, the
6:2 vow of a Nazarite, to separate himself to Jehovah.
  5 All the days of his vow of separation no razor shall
     pass over his head. He shall be holy until the days are
     fulfilled for which he separated himself to Jehovah;
     he shall let the locks of the hair of his head grow long.
Col. And He is the Head of the Body, the church; He is the
1:18 beginning, the Firstborn from the dead, that He
     Himself might have the first place in all things.

To be a Nazarite we must take care of two things. First, we
must have nothing to do with earthly pleasure. Second, we must
be absolutely under authority, absolutely under the headship.

The shaving of one's head signifies the rejecting of the headship of the Lord [cf. 1 Cor. 11:3, 6]. Spiritually speaking, for us to
shave our head means that we cast off the Lord's authority over
us. The Nazarite was to let his hair grow long (freely) [Num. 6:5];
that is, he was to remain in subjection to the Lord's headship,
wherein is the power (Judg. 16:17). (*Life-study of Numbers*, p. 58)

Today's Reading

The fallen race is a rebellious race. The rebellious nature is
still within us. Thus, it would be dangerous to be in a situation in
which there is no deputy authority. This was the reason God established human government (Gen. 9:5-6). The entire government is a deputy authority representing God's authority.

Let us apply this matter of deputy authority to the church. Is
there deputy authority in the church? If there is no deputy authority in the church, why are there elders? Recently, some have
said that there is no deputy authority in the New Testament. If
such a claim is true, why does the New Testament tell us that
there are elders in the churches? Surely, Christ is the Head, and
the authority is the Spirit, but we still need elders in the church.
Without elders, the church would be in anarchy.

There is also deputy authority in our family life. The parents
are the deputy authority to the children (Eph. 6:1), and the

husbands are the deputy authority to the wives (Eph. 5:23). Paul even says that a wife should fear her husband (Eph. 5:33). For a wife to fear her husband means that she takes him as the deputy authority. Even in a small family there is deputy authority. Then how much more should there be deputy authority in the church!

A Nazarite must deal with the rebellion in his nature. Thank God that we were created with an abundance of hair on our head, indicating that we are under authority. I can testify that it is a great blessing to be under someone, some thing, or some environment.

Children and teenagers need to be under authority. A child who is not under authority will be unruly and wild. The same is true of teenagers who are not willing to be under someone, some thing, or some environment.

It is a blessing to be under someone or some thing. It is even a blessing to be severely limited. I thank the Lord that from the day I came into the recovery, the Lord put me under someone, some thing, or some environment.

Today some are teaching that it is not necessary for believers to submit to a deputy authority, that believers should not be under anyone. This erroneous teaching is very damaging. First, it is damaging to those who teach in this way, and then it is damaging to the ones who receive such a teaching. Those who accept the teaching that the believers should not submit to deputy authority will be spoiled by this teaching. Some may even be spoiled without remedy in their youth. Therefore, it is a serious matter to teach that we should not submit to deputy authority, and it is also a serious matter to receive this teaching.

A Nazarite is a person full of hair, full of submission. With him there are a submissive spirit, standing, atmosphere, and intention. If you are such a person, there will be a great blessing for you and for your future. (*Life-study of Numbers*, pp. 59, 70-71)

Further Reading: Life-study of Numbers, msgs. 8, 10

__Enlightenment and inspiration:__ _____

_____

_____

_____

Morning Nourishment

Rom. Now the God of peace will crush Satan under your
16:20 feet shortly. The grace of our Lord Jesus be with you.
Eph.   Put on the whole armor of God that you may be able
6:11   to stand against the stratagems of the devil.
16-17 Besides all these, having taken up the shield of faith,
       with which you will be able to quench all the flaming
       darts of the evil one. And receive the helmet of sal-
       vation and the sword of the Spirit, which *Spirit* is
       the word of God.

We have seen that the church is the Body of Christ. This Body
renders supply to every member of the Body. Furthermore, this
Body also renders protection to every member. This is especially
important when it comes to the matter of spiritual warfare. Ephesians is a book that deals specifically with the Body of Christ. In
chapter six we see that spiritual warfare is something that is related to the church, not to individuals. It is the plural *you* that
must put on the whole armor of God, not the singular *you*. Satan
is not afraid of individuals. He is afraid of the church. "Upon this
rock I will build My church, and the gates of Hades shall not pre-
vail against it" (Matt. 16:18). We must meet the devil on the
ground of the Body. Even in our private prayers we should stand
by faith on the ground of the Body. Many Christians fall before the
foe because they stand alone. In fact, if we stand alone, we invite
Satan's attack. (Watchman Nee, *The Mystery of Christ*, p. 25)

Today's Reading

We must remember that the spiritual armor is for the
church, not for individuals. The Body of Christ puts on the whole
armor of God. In the Body every member has its specialty, and
all these specialties combined together form the whole armor of
God. If a brother has faith, he has the shield of faith. If another
brother has the word of God, he has the sword of the Spirit. The
whole armor of God is the totality of all the specialties of the
members. Hence, the whole armor is for the whole church, not
for individuals. Spiritual warfare is an integrated warfare of all

the members; it is not the isolated warfare of individuals. A single tree can be blown down easily, but a whole forest cannot be blown down easily. Satan likes to pick out those who are without any covering as the objects of his attacks. He looks for men who are alone and isolated. Whoever is under the protection of the Body is sheltered. One function of the Body of Christ is to protect all the members. We need the covering of the Body; otherwise, we will be constantly exposed to the enemy. An isolated individual is also prone to be deceived, so we need the covering of the Body for this as well. We should consult constantly with our fellow believers. We must not only acknowledge the need for the Body in a general way, but we should also go to our brothers and sisters in a specific way and ask for help.

We are merely members in the Body, and we need the protection of the brothers and sisters. When Moses lifted up his hands to pray for the Israelites, he needed the help of Aaron and Hur. With their help the Israelites prevailed over the Amalekites. If a man as strong as Moses needed the help of his brothers, how much more do we need the help of our brothers? Many people do things without consulting and praying with the brothers and sisters. They are ignorant of the protection of the Body, and the result is nothing but failure. We all must see the reality of the Body's protection, hide under its protection, and accept its safeguard.

This is the difference between one who has revelation of the Body and one who does not: The one who knows the Body merely as a truth may seek the counsel and covering of the Body, but he will do it as a matter of policy, not as a matter of life. When he thinks of it he will do it, but he can also forget about it. The one who has seen the Body as a reality and has entered experientially into the realm of the Body has no possibility of forgetting. His acting by the Body-principle is something spontaneous because it is his life. (Watchman Nee, *The Mystery of Christ*, pp. 25-27)

Further Reading: The Mystery of Christ, ch. 5

Enlightenment and inspiration: _____

_____

_____

Morning Nourishment

Dan.   And he will speak things against the Most High and
7:25   wear out the saints of the Most High...
2 Thes. But the Lord is faithful, who will establish you and
3:3   guard *you* from the evil one.
Rev.   And they overcame him because of the blood of the
12:11 Lamb and because of the word of their testimony...
Eph.   Therefore take up the whole armor of God that you
6:13   may be able to withstand in the evil day, and having
       done all, to stand.

If you know that Satan is wearing you out, you have to pray for God to give you a feeling of disgust, that is, a feeling of disgust and anger with Satan! Many people can get angry at men, but they cannot get angry at the devil. If others offend them, they break out in a fit of anger, but when the devil wears them out, they do not feel a thing. Paul was worn out by Satan to the extent that he became angry. Once he opened his mouth to rebuke the spirit, the spirit went away. Hence, we must not keep our mouth shut all the time; we have to declare something. It would be wonderful if God's children would become angry with Satan and rebuke him. If anyone becomes angry with Satan, we will say, "Hallelujah, this is wonderful!" Some people are very weak; they allow Satan to wear them out. This is too poor. God's children should become angry with Satan. They need to be disgusted with him. Once they become angry and disgusted, everything will be set right. (*The Collected Works of Watchman Nee*, vol. 38, p. 390)

Today's Reading

God's children should stand up to reject Satan in disgust; they should rebuke Satan. Some people have never experienced deliverance or release because they still have the "strength" to endure. A man who endures Satan's wearing out and allows Satan to waste his energy, joy, and spirit has fallen into Satan's trap. We are not saying that we should be angry with those men whom Satan has used.... But we should oppose and reject the strategies and methods of Satan. If we oppose Satan's work, we will be freed and liberated.

The power to reject Satan comes from realizing his pressure. Some believers have been deceived and attacked by Satan. They withstand it and oppose it, yet they do not feel that they have any strength....This is because we have not seen Satan's pressure. Whether or not we can reject Satan depends on whether we are disgusted with him. If we are not sufficiently disgusted with him, our speaking to him will be like speaking to the air; it will not produce any effect. But when we truly become disgusted and angry with him, the anger will become our strength, and the minute we open our mouth, he will go away.

Such a feeling of disgust comes from revelation. Once we see that Satan is wearing us out, we must oppose him. Once we see this, Satan cannot do anything more; he will realize his hopelessness. May the Lord be merciful to us so that we see Satan's wearing-out work. As long as we tolerate and endure him, his work will continue. But the minute we feel disgusted and become angry with him, Satan will go away. We must realize that no other kind of withstanding will work. Satan will withdraw only when we withstand him with our words. If we do not see this and allow him to go on, he will not stop. When we see that Satan is doing the work and plotting everything, we must say, "I do not want this. I oppose this." God will then bless our withstanding, and it will become effectual.

Finally, let us read Ephesians 6:13. Paul said, "Having done all, to stand." We must stand and not allow Satan to continue wearing us out. May the Lord open our eyes to see Satan's wearing-out work on God's children. We have to reject this, and we have to speak up. We have to say, "I reject this. I oppose this. I do not accept this wearing out." We must not accept any kind of wearing out from Satan; we should oppose it and reject it. If we do this, we will witness the Lord's deliverance and release, and we will be freed from Satan's wearing-out work. (*The Collected Works of Watchman Nee*, vol. 38, pp. 391-392)

Further Reading: The Collected Works of Watchman Nee, vol. 38, ch. 52;
    Life-study of Exodus, msg. 28; *Life-study of Psalms*, msg. 23

Enlightenment and inspiration: _____

_____

_____

_____

Morning Nourishment

Eph. And raised *us* up together with *Him* and seated *us* to-
2:6 gether with *Him* in the heavenlies in Christ Jesus.
6:12 For our wrestling is not against blood and flesh but
against the rulers, against the authorities, against the
world-rulers of this darkness, against the spiritual
forces of evil in the heavenlies.
2 Tim. No one serving as a soldier entangles himself with the
2:4 affairs of this life, that he may please the one who enlisted *him.*
4:7 I have fought the good fight; I have finished the course;
I have kept the faith.

If our eyes have been opened by the Lord, we will see that the
nature of our work in serving the Lord is that of warfare. All our
spiritual work, whether it be delivering men from sin, from the
world, from illness, or from problems, has an ultimate goal: to rescue men out of the power of Satan and drive out the satanic power
of darkness from within men, so that men might be gained by God
and gained even more by God. Thus, God's name will be sanctified
in men, God's kingdom will reach unto men, His will shall be done
in men, and thereby His glory will be manifested upon men.
Therefore, the nature of all this work is that of spiritual warfare.
(*The Experience of Life,* pp. 366-367)

Today's Reading

There is only one kind of people who can engage in spiritual
warfare—those who have received salvation, have been raised
from death, and are now sitting with Christ in the heavens. Only
this kind of men can attack the enemy in the air from a transcen-
dent position in the heavens. Therefore, in order to engage in spiritual warfare we must keep the heavenly position. Whenever we
are not heavenly enough, whenever we lose our heavenly condition, everything is finished. If our gospel is powerless, it is because
we are not heavenly enough; we ourselves are earthly, and we are
using earthly methods or fleshly weapons to preach the gospel. As
a result, we may get some saved, but their condition will be

muddled, and they will be unable to be completely delivered out of the power of Satan. If we really desire to deliver men out of Satan's power so that they are not only saved, but completely delivered from the hands of Satan, we who are preaching the gospel must be men who are sitting in the heavens and keeping the ascended position.

The same principle applies in edifying the saints. If we lose the position of ascension, we can neither supply nor help the saints. If the messages we preach are mere doctrines and the fellowship we give mere knowledge, containing no element of warfare, the most we can impart is teachings for the mentality and stirring in the emotions; we cannot deliver people out of the power of Satan and turn them to God in a practical way. Therefore, if we want our work to have the effect of war, work which is able to deliver men from Satan's hands, we must keep the position of ascension and live continually in the condition of the heavens. This is an extremely important secret.

Only those who live in the realm of the heavens can deal with the power of darkness in the air and chase the devil out. The help, the deliverance, which we afford others is based solely on that part which is of the heavenly nature in us. The extent to which we chase out the power of darkness is directly dependent on our heavenly condition. If we have more element of the heavens, we can engage more in spiritual warfare. If we have only a little element of the heavens, we can by no means have much element of spiritual warfare. The two are in direct proportion to one another. When a man has utterly reached the heavenly realm, his whole being, living, works, and actions are spiritual warfare. He is able to chase out the power of darkness from every place to which he comes and from all the people whom he meets. Therefore, when we in our experience have reached the position of ascension and are able to reign, that will be the time we can fight for the kingdom of God, recover the lost earth for God, and bring in the kingdom of God. (*The Experience of Life,* pp. 368-369)

Further Reading: The Experience of Life, chs. 16-18; *Life-study of Leviticus,* msg. 26; *Christ Our Portion,* chs. 1-2; *Living in the Spirit,* ch. 5

Enlightenment and inspiration: _____
_____
_____
_____

Hymns, #885

1   Fight the battle in the Body,
        Never fight it on your own;
    With the Body to the Head joined,
        Fight the battle on the throne.

        Fight the battle in the Body!
            By the virtue of the Head;
        Standing firmly with the Body,
            Into vict'ry you'll be led.

2   For the Body is God's armor,
        Not for anyone alone;
    When you wrestle in the Body,
        All its benefits you own.

3   'Tis the Church on Christ established
        Satan shall not overpow'r;
    'Tis the Body built together
        Which resists the evil pow'r.

4   In the Body, by the Headship,
        Sitting in the heavenlies,
    Struggle with the wicked spirits
        And the principalities.

5   As a member of the Body,
        With the brethren stand for God;
    Praying always in the Spirit,
        Claim the vict'ry through the Blood.

6   In the heav'nlies more than conqu'ror,
        In the power of His might,
    As a soldier in the army,
        In the Lord the battle fight.

7   Keep on wrestling in the Body,
        Mighty vict'ry you will see,
    Bind and loose, God's will fulfilling,
        And the foes your food will be.

Composition for prophecy with main point and sub-points: _____

_____
_____
_____
_____
_____
_____
_____
_____
_____
_____
_____
_____
_____
_____
_____
_____
_____
_____
_____
_____
_____
_____
_____
_____
_____
_____
_____
_____
_____
_____
_____
_____
_____
_____
_____
_____
_____

Expression

Scripture Reading: Exo. 40:34-35; 1 Kings 8:10-11; Eph. 3:21; 5:26-27; Rev. 4:3; 21:10-11, 18

Day 1 & Day 2

I. **The Lord's recovery is the recovery of the expression of God; the central line in the divine revelation is that the Triune God desires to express Himself in humanity (Gen. 1:26; 2:7; Isa. 43:7; 2 Cor. 4:7; cf. Dan. 5:23):**

A. The entire Old Testament is composed of nine great men (Adam, Abel, Enosh, Enoch, Noah, Abraham, Isaac, Jacob, and Joseph) plus the tabernacle and the temple as God's dwelling place for God's expression (Gen. 1:26; 4:4, 26; 5:24; 6:8; 17:1-5; 24:4; 28:10-13; 50:26; Exo. 40:34-35; 1 Kings 8:1-11).

B. The entire New Testament is composed of a unique man who was God's tabernacle and temple plus the church as the enlargement of this unique man to be God's dwelling place for God's expression (John 1:14; 2:19-21; 1 Cor. 3:16-17; 1 Tim. 3:15; Heb. 3:6; Eph. 3:19-21; Rev. 21:3, 22, 10-11).

Day 3

II. **The history of the tabernacle and the Ark portrays the desire of God's heart, the desolation of the church, and the recovery of the church for God's testimony, God's expression (Exo. 25:9-10; 26:26-30; 40:38):**

A. As the center and content of the tabernacle, the Ark signifies Christ as the center and content of the church as God's tabernacle, God's house, for God's corporate expression (25:22; 40:21; Col. 2:9; Eph. 2:21-22; 1 Tim. 3:15).

B. In the first stage of its history, the Ark was in the tabernacle; this signifies that in the first stage of its history, the normal church was the expression of Christ, and Christ was the content of the church (Exo. 40:34-35; Acts 9:31).

C. Due to Israel's degradation, the Ark was captured by the Philistines and was separated from the tabernacle, leaving the tabernacle an empty vessel without the proper content; this signifies that in the second stage the church became degraded and lost the reality and presence of Christ (1 Sam. 3—4; Rev. 3:20):

1. In their degradation Israel should have repented, made a thorough confession, returned to God from their idols, and inquired of God as to what He wanted them to do; instead, having no heart for God's desire or for His eternal economy, they exercised their superstition to trust in the Ark based on their past victories (Num. 10:35; Josh. 6; cf. Phil. 3:13-14).

2. In their degradation they offended God to the uttermost; eventually, instead of the Ark saving Israel, the Ark itself was captured and the glory of God departed from Israel (1 Sam. 4:11a, 21-22; Psa. 78:61).

3. The Ark typifies Christ as the embodiment of God and as the presence of the Triune God with His people for the carrying out of His economy to establish His kingdom on earth; to bring out the Ark was to bring out the presence of God (Num. 10:33-36; 1 Sam. 4:4).

4. The children of Israel had no thought or concern for God's economy, and their bringing out the Ark indicated that they were usurping God, even forcing Him to go out with them for their safety, peace, rest, and profit.

5. Today men are replacing God's testimony with man's need; when man's need replaces God's testimony, degradation begins and problems arise.

6. In principle, we do the same thing whenever we pray for our prosperity without any consideration of God's economy; instead of

usurping God, we should pray, live, and be
persons, like Samuel, who are according to
God's heart and for His economy (1 Sam.
2:30b, 35; cf. 1 Kings 8:48; Jer. 32:39).

D. Later, the Ark was recovered and brought first to
the house of Abinidab at Kiriath-jearim, where it
remained for twenty years (1 Sam. 6:2—7:2), and
then to the house of Obed-edom the Gittite, where
it stayed for three months (2 Sam. 6:1-11; cf.
1 Sam. 1:24; Josh. 18:1); this signifies that beginning from the second century a number of
"Obed-edoms" were raised up, who had the Lord's
presence (the Ark) but did not have the proper
church life as the expression of Christ (the tabernacle).

Day 4   E. David moved the Ark from Obed-edom's house to
a tent that he had prepared for it in his own city, at
Mount Zion, the choicest place in Jerusalem
(2 Sam. 6:12-19; 1 Chron. 15:1—16:1); this signifies that other believers who, like David, cared for
God's interests, attempted to practice the church
life according to their own choice, not according to
God's revelation; these believers had Christ, but
they had Him with an improper practice of the
church life (typified by David's tent in Jerusalem).

F. Finally, after Solomon finished the building of the
temple in Jerusalem, the Ark was moved into the
Holy of Holies in the temple for a full recovery of
the normal situation; today in His recovery the
Lord is working to restore the normal condition of
Christ within the proper church as His expression
(1 Kings 8:1-11; Eph. 3:16-21).

Day 5 III. **The history of the destruction of the temple
and the city of God due to Israel's degradation
and the rebuilding of the temple and the city
with its wall typify God's recovery of the degraded church for His glory, His expression:**
A. Solomon, the very one who had built the temple,
took the lead to build up the high places again;

these high places were related to lust, ambition, and idolatry, resulting in division (1 Kings 11:1-8, 43; 12:31):

1. Solomon was a wise man but not a spiritual man; a man of capability, not a man of life; a man whose wisdom was a gift, not a measure of life.

2. Capability apart from life is like a snake, poisoning God's people (cf. Exo. 4:2-4); life is like a dove, supplying God's people with life (John 1:32).

B. God's people in their degradation eventually set up idols in the temple and in their hearts; God's glory, His expression, is versus idols; an idol in our heart is anything within us that we love more than the Lord and that replaces the Lord in our life (Ezek. 2:3; 8:2-4, 10; 11:23; 14:3, 5; 40:1; 43:2, 10; 1 John 5:21).

C. After the destruction of the temple and the city because of Israel's idolatry, the temple and the city with its wall were rebuilt by the returned captives for the glory of God, the expression of God (Ezra 3:6b-13; 6:13-15; Neh. 4:1-23).

Day 6 IV. **The wall of the city is for the expression of God; thus, to "build up the wall" is to build up the church as the expression of God (Rev. 4:3; 21:11, 18-19):**

A. In order to express God, we need to be saved from our natural disposition and from self-likeness by living a mingled life with the Divine Trinity in the blending life of the entire Body of Christ (Rom. 5:10; Lev. 2:4-5; 1 Cor. 12:24).

B. In order to express God, we need to be daily sanctified and renewed by the washing of the water in the word to be presented to Christ, our Bridegroom, as His pure, glorious, God-expressing bride (Heb. 2:10-11; Eph. 5:26-27; 3:21).

Morning Nourishment

Gen. And God said, Let Us make man in Our image, accord-
1:26 ing to Our likeness; and let them have dominion...
  2:9 And out of the ground Jehovah God caused to grow ev-
       ery tree that is pleasant to the sight and good for food,
       as well as the tree of life in the middle of the garden...
1 Kings And the priests were not able to stand and minister be-
8:11 cause of the cloud, for the glory of Jehovah filled the
       house of Jehovah.

The central thing in God's revelation is that God wants to be
expressed....The invisible God desires to be seen through an in-
strument, through humanity, the very man created by Him.
Man and the entire universe were created for this purpose.

Genesis 1:26 and 27 occupy a strong place in the Bible, telling
us that when God was going to make man it seemed that the Triune God held a conference. Verse 26 says let "Us" make man....
The decision was made to create man in Their own image and
after Their own likeness.

In the second chapter of the Bible, after man was created in
the image of God, God brought him to the tree of life. This is a
strong indication that the man created by God did not have the
divine life of God. So God brought him to the tree of life, indicating that God wanted him to take the tree of life in order to receive the divine life of God into himself....Man was made for
God's expression. We should not express ourselves. We should
express God because we were made in God's image and after
God's likeness. (*Concerning the Lord's Recovery*, pp. 18-20)

Today's Reading

The central line in the entire Bible is God's expression. In
Genesis there is the record of nine great men who are land-
marks in the human history: Adam, Abel, Enosh, Enoch, Noah,
Abraham, Isaac, Jacob, and Joseph. Adam was first, and he became fallen. Abel came back to God taking God's way of redemption and salvation. Following him was Enosh, who realized that
fallen man is so weak, fragile, and good for nothing. So he had no

trust in himself, but he called on the name of Jehovah. [Enoch] walked with God. This indicates a little improvement. This is not just to call upon the name of the Lord, but to walk with Him....Noah not only walked with the Lord, but he also worked with the Lord and worked for the Lord. He built the ark with the Lord and for the Lord.

Abraham...was called out of the idolatrous land. His son, Isaac, and his grandson, Jacob, continued after him. With Jacob something happened as a further development of God's expression. When he was escaping from his brother...(Gen. 28), during the night he had a dream in which he saw a ladder reaching into the heavens with the angels descending and ascending upon it. Jacob called that place the gate of heaven and the house of God, Bethel. That was God's dwelling place. The next morning he anointed his stone pillow with oil and called it Bethel, the house of God. This is very meaningful. God gave this wanderer a dream showing him that God desired to have Bethel, a house on this earth. Humanly speaking nothing can express you so much as your house. When you look at people's dwelling places, right away you can realize what kind of people they are. God wants a dwelling place on this earth to express Himself.

[Joseph] ruled on the earth for God's expression. Eventually all of Jacob's descendants fell into Egypt. After four hundred years, God brought the children of Israel out of Egypt to Mount Sinai where He revealed the tabernacle to them. God wanted them to be His dwelling place that God might be expressed among them and through them. Later, that tabernacle was enlarged into a temple. The tabernacle was a traveling house of God, but the temple became a settled house upon this earth. This covers the entire Old Testament....God had nine men from Adam to Joseph who expressed Him in a limited way. Then in the second book of the Bible, Exodus, God got a collective people who became His expression in a full way. (*Concerning the Lord's Recovery*, pp. 20-21)

Further Reading: Concerning the Lord's Recovery, chs. 2-3

Enlightenment and inspiration: _____

_____

_____

_____

Morning Nourishment

John **And the Word became flesh and tabernacled among**
1:14 **us (and we beheld His glory, glory as of the only Be-**
gotten from the Father), full of grace and reality.
Eph. **In whom you also are being built together into a**
2:22 **dwelling place of God in spirit.**
1 Tim. **...The house of God, which is the church of the liv-**
3:15-16 **ing God, the pillar and base of the truth. And con-**
fessedly, great is the mystery of godliness: He who
was manifested in the flesh...

The New Testament began not with nine great men but with
one unique man. This man is wonderful. He is both God and man.
He is God in the heavens becoming a man on this earth. So this
man joined the heavens to the earth and brought the earth up to
join the heavens. He was surely the ladder which Jacob saw in his
dream (Gen. 28:12). This ladder is the very gate of heaven and
also the house of God, Bethel. While He was on this earth He was
tabernacling....He was really a traveling tabernacle. But He was
God's dwelling place. As God's temple He was destroyed, and He
raised Himself up in the way of enlargement. In His resurrection
He raised us up with Himself....All of us were resurrected with
Him and became the temple. The temple was on a bigger scale
than the tabernacle....This temple today is all over the globe. This
is the church....[The New Testament] contains a unique man
who was God's tabernacle and the church which is the enlargement of this unique man as God's dwelling place on the earth.
(*Concerning the Lord's Recovery,* pp. 31-32)

Today's Reading

In the New Testament the first person is Jesus Christ. He was
God becoming a man, and He became a tabernacle (John 1:14).
When He was on this earth, He was tabernacling among men. He
was God's dwelling place. The model of the tabernacle was in Exo-
dus, and the genuine tabernacle, Jesus Christ, is in the Gospel of
John. One day this tabernacle told the Jews that if they destroyed
Him, He would raise up the temple within three days. Of course,

they did destroy Him by crucifying Him on the cross, and He did raise Himself up in an enlarged way. In the raised-up temple, the church, we all are there. This is God's expression.

Ephesians on the one hand tells us that we are builded together into a temple of God to express God, and on the other hand that the church is the Body of Christ, the fullness of the One who fills all in all (Eph. 2:21-22; 1:23). What is the fullness? The fullness is just the expression. If a glass has water in it, but it is not overflowing there is not the fullness. It is not until the water flows over the brim of the glass that there is the overflowing, the fullness. This fullness is the expression of the water. We are all vessels to contain God (Rom. 9:21, 23). If we have only a little bit of God and no overflowing, there is no fullness,...no expression. The church should be a vessel that is full of God and even overflowing with God;...that is the fullness. That fullness is the very expression of God....Just to be the dwelling place of God is not adequate. We must be the fullness of God. Then the church can express God. When we overflow God, we have the fullness of the One who fills all in all. Then we become the full expression of the all-inclusive and wonderful God.

Paul, in 1 Timothy 3:15-16, tells us that the house of God is the church of the living God which is the pillar and base of the truth and which also is the manifestation of this all-inclusive God in human flesh. When we come together with the fullness of God, an outsider would realize that this is the manifestation of God in the flesh. Although we are flesh, we overflow God. Among us is the manifestation of the invisible God, and this manifestation is the expression of God.

This expression which is the church today will consummate to the uttermost in the New Jerusalem, which will be the eternal tabernacle. All of God's redeemed people will be one corporate entity, the New Jerusalem, to express God for eternity. (*Concerning the Lord's Recovery,* pp. 21-23)

Further Reading: Concerning the Lord's Recovery, chs. 2-3

Enlightenment and inspiration: _____

_____

_____

_____

Morning Nourishment

Exo. And you shall put into the Ark the Testimony which I
25:16 shall give you.
40:35 And Moses was not able to enter the Tent of Meeting,
       because the cloud settled on it and the glory of Jeho-
       vah filled the tabernacle.
Rev.   And he...showed me the holy city, Jerusalem, coming
21:10-11 down out of heaven from God, having the glory of
       God....

Because the law, God's testimony, was placed in the Ark (Exo.
25:16, 21; Deut. 10:1-5), the Ark was called the Ark of the Testimony (Exo. 25:22; 26:33-34); and because the Ark was in the
tabernacle, the tabernacle was called the Tabernacle of the Testimony (38:21; Num. 1:50, 53). As the embodiment of God's testimony, the Ark typifies Christ as the embodiment of God (Col.
2:9). The Ark as a type of Christ indicates that God's redeemed
people can contact God and enjoy God in Christ and through
Christ (John 14:6; Heb. 10:19-20).

As the center and content of the tabernacle, the Ark also signifies Christ as the center and content of the church as God's tabernacle, God's house (Eph. 2:21-22; 1 Tim. 3:15). The fact that the
Ark is the item first mentioned in the vision of the tabernacle and
its furniture indicates that it occupies the place of preeminence
(cf. Col. 1:18). It also indicates that the church, the Body of Christ,
typified by the tabernacle, comes out of Christ, typified by the
Ark. (Note 1 on Exodus 25:10, Recovery Version)

Today's Reading

In the Old Testament times the house of God was the house
of Israel, represented here by the tabernacle and later by the
temple. At the end of Genesis an individual Israel was produced
as a miniature of God's house to express God and exercise His authority. At the end of Exodus a corporate Israel was produced as
God's house to express God and represent Him by exercising His
authority on earth. The goal of God's eternal purpose is to have a
corporate people to be His dwelling place for His expression and

representation in eternity. The books of Genesis and Exodus together consummate with God's tabernacle, His dwelling place, filled with His glory (Exo. 40:34). Likewise, the entire Bible consummates in the New Jerusalem as the eternal tabernacle of God filled with the glory of God (Rev. 21:2-3, 10-11) and exercising God's authority for His divine administration in eternity (22:1, 5). (Note 2 on Exodus 40:38, Recovery Version)

In 1 Samuel 4 the elders of Israel were actually usurping God. ...The children of Israel had no thought of or concern for God's economy, and their bringing out the ark indicated that they were usurping God for their safety, peace, rest, and profit. They were usurping God, even forcing Him, to go out with them. Today many Christians usurp God by praying for their prosperity, health, or family without any consideration of God's economy....Instead of usurping God, we must pray, live, and be persons according to God's heart and for His economy.

Eventually, the Ark of God, which had been with the children of Israel for at least 400 years, was captured by the winning Philistines, indicating that the glory had departed from Israel (1 Sam. 4:9-22). From that time the Ark began to have a history within the history of Israel.

God protected His holiness, not allowing the Philistines or the people of Beth-shemesh to do whatever they liked with the Ark. Eventually, the people of Beth-shemesh asked the people of Kiriath-jearim to come and take the Ark (6:20-21), and the Ark remained there for twenty years (7:1-2). Although the Ark returned to Israel and was under the care of the proper priesthood, the Ark still did not go back to the tabernacle at Shiloh. This was an abnormal situation....The Ark remained in Kiriath-jearim for twenty years until all the house of Israel lamented after Jehovah (v. 2). (*Life-study of 1 & 2 Samuel*, pp. 22-23, 26)

Further Reading: Life-study of 1 & 2 Samuel, msgs. 3-4; Messages Given during the Resumption of Watchman Nee's Ministry, ch. 41; The Vision of the Building of the Church, ch. 6

Enlightenment and inspiration: _____

_____

_____

Morning Nourishment

Josh. 18:1	And the whole assembly of the children of Israel gathered together at Shiloh, and they set up the Tent of Meeting there; and the land was subdued before them.
2 Sam. 6:12	And it was told King David, saying, Jehovah has blessed the house of Obed-edom and all that he has because of the Ark of God. So David went and brought up the Ark of God from the house of Obed-edom into the city of David with rejoicing.
1 Kings 8:13	I have surely built You a lofty house, a place for You to dwell in forever.

The history of the tabernacle with the Ark is vitally important if we would realize God's desire concerning His building. In the previous chapter we saw that when the tabernacle was completed, six major things followed. Firstly, the glory of God Himself appeared on this earth and filled the tabernacle. The glory of God's presence was clearly seen by His people—this is no small matter. Secondly, God spoke from the tabernacle. To receive God's word we must come to the building of God. Thirdly, a priestly service or a priesthood was formed. Fourthly, this priesthood was also an army to fight the battle for God. Fifthly, all the battles were won with the purpose of gaining the ground for God's building. And lastly, the tabernacle was set up as a worship center in a place called Shiloh (Josh. 18:1). From that time, any person seeking the Lord, such as Samuel's parents (1 Sam. 1:3-9), had a definite place to go. How wonderful the situation was! But it did not last long. (*The Vision of God's Building*, p. 112)

Today's Reading

The situation [became] abnormal: the tabernacle with the altar was in Shiloh, but the Ark was in Kirjath-jearim.…The abnormal state of Ark and tabernacle in separation lasted for at least twenty years.…The desire of God's heart was for His building. Finally, God found David, a man after the desire of His own heart (1 Sam. 13:14).…Upon taking the throne as king, practically the first thing in David's heart was to care for the Ark [Psalm 132].

David followed God with a sincere heart, but when he sent for the Ark he lacked enlightenment. He had a heart for God, but not the light from God; so he acted wrongly....Upon the incident of Uzzah and the resulting frustration, David left the Ark with a man named Obed-edom (2 Sam. 6:1-10)....But after a short time, he was informed that God had greatly blessed Obed-edom. David was moved, so much so that he proceeded to bring the Ark from the house of Obed-edom into his own city (2 Sam. 6:11-12),...[but] this time he realized that the Ark should not be borne by a cart, but by living persons,...by those who were designated, separated and holy. Only the priests could bear the Ark (1 Chron. 15:1-15).... David finally succeeded in bringing the Ark to Mount Zion, the choicest spot in Jerusalem (1 Chron. 15:25; 16:1).

On Mount Zion David had prepared a tent to contain the Ark. Was this all right? No, it was not absolutely right. With this arrangement there was not yet complete satisfaction.

[Then] the temple built by Solomon was not according to any human design, for God had clearly shown David the pattern of the building (1 Chron. 28:11-19)....Thus Solomon built the temple on the proper ground according to the pattern revealed to his father David.

Then the glory of God filled the temple just as it did the tabernacle (1 Kings 8:10-11). Again the glory of God's presence was seen on this earth, but this time it was in an increased portion. God's doing is victorious! God moves on in steady progress! Regardless of how much the enemy would and could do to damage and frustrate God's building on this earth, God brings forth something better, something larger than what has been damaged and frustrated. The enemy damaged the tabernacle and frustrated the recovery of its normal condition, but eventually God built a larger dwelling, the temple, in a more normal condition. God can never be defeated in His purpose! (*The Vision of God's Building*, pp. 114-120)

Further Reading: The Vision of God's Building, ch. 10

Enlightenment and inspiration: _____

_____

_____

_____

Morning Nourishment

1 Kings 11:7-8	Then Solomon built a high place to Chemosh the detestable thing of Moab in the mountain that is before Jerusalem and to Molech the detestable thing of the children of Ammon. And so he did for all his foreign wives, who burned incense and offered sacrifices to their gods.
2 Chron. 36:18-19	And all the vessels of the house of God, great and small, and the treasures of the house of Jehovah and the treasures of the king and of his princes, all these he brought to Babylon. And they burned down the house of God; and they broke down the wall of Jerusalem and burned down all its palaces with fire, and all its precious vessels *were given up* to destruction.

[The high places were the] places where the Gentile peoples worshipped their idols. When the children of Israel entered the land of Canaan to possess it, God commanded them to destroy all the high places of the nations (Num. 33:52). In 1 Kings 11:7 Solomon, the very one who had built the temple according to God's desire on the ground of the oneness of God's people, took the lead to build up the high places once again. These high places were related to fornication and idolatry. Solomon's setting up of the high places was especially connected with the indulgence of lust in his loving many foreign women. (Note 1 on 1 Kings 11:7, Recovery Version)

Today's Reading

The tragedy of Israel's history (1 Kings 11) was due to Solomon's indulgence of lust and worship of idols....In 11:1-8 we have a record of Solomon's fall....Solomon's fall was in his indulgence of his lust...(vv. 1-3). In having so many wives and concubines Solomon was most foolish....Solomon's fall was also in his forsaking God, who appeared to him twice (v. 9), and in worshipping the Gentile idols through the seducing of the foreign women he loved (vv. 4-8).

Solomon's decease after reigning over all Israel for forty years (vv. 41-43) was in a gloomy disappointment. His glory fell off like the flower of grass (Matt. 6:29; 1 Pet. 1:24), and his splendid career became "vanity of vanities," as he had preached (Eccl. 1:2). However, what God did through him as a type of Christ remains forever. We, therefore, need to discern between what Solomon was in his personal life and what he was as a type of Christ.

Under the light of the spiritual life, we can see that Solomon was a wise man but not a spiritual one; a man of capability, not one of life; a man whose wisdom was a gift, not a measure of life. The careers he accomplished were evidences of his capacity from the God-given gift of wisdom, not manifestations of the ability of the maturity of life.

In the Lord's recovery we should first take care of life. Then to some extent and in a certain sense we need capability. In the church our capability should be the manifestation of the maturity of life. Capability apart from life is like a snake, poisoning the church; life is like a dove, supplying the church with life. Instead of being today's Solomon, we should be "doves" with the proper measure of life.

Solomon's enjoyment of the God-given good land reached the highest level through his God-given gift. However, due to his dwarf measurement in the maturity of the spiritual life, he was cut off from the enjoyment of the good land in God's economy, in his unbridled indulgence of his lust in sex. His father David, a man according to God's heart, failed in this gross and ugly sin— the indulgence of sexual lust. Solomon's failure in this satanic temptation was much greater than his father's, beyond people's imagination. This caused him and his descendants to lose more than ninety percent of their kingdom and caused the people of God's elect to suffer division and confusions among themselves throughout quite a number of generations. They lost the God-given land and became captives in the foreign lands of idol worship....What a warning and an alarm this should be to us! We must be careful. Even a little failure in the indulgence of lust can damage the church and kill the splendid aspects of the church life. (*Life-study of 1 & 2 Kings,* pp. 45-47)

Further Reading: Life-study of 1 & 2 Kings, msg. 7

Enlightenment and inspiration: _____

_____

_____

_____

Morning Nourishment

Rev. And He who was sitting was like a jasper stone...in
4:3   appearance...
21:10-11 And he carried me away in spirit onto a great and
high mountain and showed me the holy city,
Jerusalem, coming down out of heaven from God,
having the glory of God. Her light was like a most
precious stone, like a jasper stone, as clear as
crystal.
18 And the building work of its wall was jasper...

[In the New Jerusalem, the] function of the wall is to express God. God's appearance is like jasper and the light of the New Jerusalem is like jasper, so the whole city will express God. God the Father is the gold as the base; God the Son is the gates to bring people in; and God the Spirit transforms people to express God. The base of gold is something within, but the wall can be seen. This wall is in the color of the stone that signifies God, that is, jasper. Revelation 21:11 reveals that the city's glory is like the glory of jasper. That is God's appearance. Today, the function of the Body of Christ which consummates in the New Jerusalem is to express Christ. (*The Application of the Interpretation of the New Jerusalem to the Seeking Believers*, p. 35)

Today's Reading

Revelation 21:18a tells us that the wall was built with jasper, signifying the appearance of God (4:3a) for His expression. God sitting on His throne looks like jasper and the entire wall, a great and high wall, is built with jasper. Also, the first foundation of the wall is jasper. Jasper, according to Revelation 21:11, is "a most precious stone...clear as crystal." Its color must be dark green, which signifies life in its richness. God's appearance being like jasper means that His very appearance is life in its richness. Jasper is the appearance of God, which will also be the appearance of the holy city, New Jerusalem (Rev. 21:11). The entire city, in appearance, looks the same as God. We all need to see the wonderful picture portrayed in this city. The center of the city is

God on the throne who appears as jasper and the circumference of the city is its wall which is built with jasper. This means that the entire city from its center to its circumference is an expression of the very God of life in His richness.

The wall of the New Jerusalem also implies the expression of God. The great wall is the unique expression of the jasper God, and the jasper God is expressed in the jasper city through the jasper wall. A picture such as this is better than one thousand words. When we look at this city which is in the appearance of God for His expression, we can see that today's Christianity does not match this. With the denominations there are too many different kinds of expressions, but in the church life, which will consummate in the coming New Jerusalem, there is only one expression—the expression of the divine image through transformation and building.

This expression of God in the New Jerusalem will be a testimony of Jesus. On the one hand, the book of Revelation gives us the revelation of Christ (1:1), and on the other hand it shows us the testimony of Jesus (1:9; 12:17; 19:10; 20:4). The expression of the greenish wall is the testimony of Jesus. Jesus was the embodiment of the Triune God. While He was on this earth He expressed the Triune God. The New Jerusalem will be His enlargement, His increase, and His expansion to express Him as God's embodiment, and this is the testimony of Jesus. Today every local church must be such a testimony, but it depends upon the degree of transformation and building. The transformation and the building are the basic factors to have the testimony of Jesus expressing the Triune God. (*God's New Testament Economy,* pp. 379, 383-384)

Further Reading: The Application of the Interpretation of the New Jerusalem to the Seeking Believers, msg. 3; *God's New Testament Economy,* ch. 36; *Life-study of Romans,* msgs. 44-45; *The Experience and Growth in Life,* msgs. 23-24; *Messages to the Trainees in Fall 1990,* ch. 6

Enlightenment and inspiration: _____
_____
_____

Hymns, #838

1 Thy blueprint, Lord, I treasure dear,
  It shows Thy tabernacle real,
  It tells how Thou wouldst have it built,
  How Thou Thy glory wouldst reveal.

2 The ark's the center of the tent,
  The tent is but its resting-place:
  In it the ten commandments are,
  And in the tent it ever stays.

3 The ark the God-man, Christ, displays—
  God mixed with man, as gold, wood meet;
  The law is God's expression full,
  Which dwells in Christ the Son complete.

4 Thus Christ's the center of the Church,
  Which is to Him a resting-place;
  In Christ the Father ever dwells,
  And in the Church, Christ's dwelling-place.

5 The tent's the increase of the ark,
  Both are of wood with gold o'erlaid;
  The Church the increase is of Christ,
  God blent with man here too displayed.

6 The boards when joined support the tent
  On silver sockets standing sure;
  Gold overlaid, with golden rings
  And interlocking bars, secure.

7 The Church is thus the gathered saints,
  On Christ's redemption standing sure;
  In life divine, by Spirit bound,
  Together built and framed secure.

8 The tent's four-layered cover shows
  The Christ of God in every phase;
  God's glory thus is signified,
  Covering His holy dwelling-place.

9 Covered by such a glorious Christ,
  All saints together knit may be;
  Enjoying all He is for them,
  In Him they're builded gloriously.

10 The law is placed within the ark,
  The ark within the tent doth rest;
  So God in Christ within the Church
  His wondrous glory manifests.

Composition for prophecy with main point and sub-points: _____

_____
_____
_____
_____
_____
_____
_____
_____
_____
_____
_____
_____
_____
_____
_____
_____
_____
_____
_____
_____
_____
_____
_____
_____
_____
_____
_____
_____
_____
_____
_____
_____
_____
_____
_____
_____
_____
_____
_____
_____

Reading Schedule for the Recovery Version of the New Testament with Footnotes

Wk.	Lord's Day	Monday	Tuesday	Wednesday	Thursday	Friday	Saturday
1	☐ Matt 1:1-2	☐ 1:3-7	☐ 1:8-17	☐ 1:18-25	☐ 2:1-23	☐ 3:1-6	☐ 3:7-17
2	☐ 4:1-11	☐ 4:12-25	☐ 5:1-4	☐ 5:5-12	☐ 5:13-20	☐ 5:21-26	☐ 5:27-48
3	☐ 6:1-8	☐ 6:9-18	☐ 6:19-34	☐ 7:1-12	☐ 7:13-29	☐ 8:1-13	☐ 8:14-22
4	☐ 8:23-34	☐ 9:1-13	☐ 9:14-17	☐ 9:18-34	☐ 9:35—10:5	☐ 10:6-25	☐ 10:26-42
5	☐ 11:1-15	☐ 11:16-30	☐ 12:1-14	☐ 12:15-32	☐ 12:33-42	☐ 12:43—13:2	☐ 13:3-12
6	☐ 13:13-30	☐ 13:31-43	☐ 13:44-58	☐ 14:1-13	☐ 14:14-21	☐ 14:22-36	☐ 15:1-20
7	☐ 15:21-31	☐ 15:32-39	☐ 16:1-12	☐ 16:13-20	☐ 16:21-28	☐ 17:1-13	☐ 17:14-27
8	☐ 18:1-14	☐ 18:15-22	☐ 18:23-35	☐ 19:1-15	☐ 19:16-30	☐ 20:1-16	☐ 20:17-34
9	☐ 21:1-11	☐ 21:12-22	☐ 21:23-32	☐ 21:33-46	☐ 22:1-22	☐ 22:23-33	☐ 22:34-46
10	☐ 23:1-12	☐ 23:13-39	☐ 24:1-14	☐ 24:15-31	☐ 24:32-51	☐ 25:1-13	☐ 25:14-30
11	☐ 25:31-46	☐ 26:1-16	☐ 26:17-35	☐ 26:36-46	☐ 26:47-64	☐ 26:65-75	☐ 27:1-26
12	☐ 27:27-44	☐ 27:45-56	☐ 27:57—28:15	☐ 28:16-20	☐ Mark 1:1	☐ 1:2-6	☐ 1:7-13
13	☐ 1:14-28	☐ 1:29-45	☐ 2:1-12	☐ 2:13-28	☐ 3:1-19	☐ 3:20-35	☐ 4:1-25
14	☐ 4:26-41	☐ 5:1-20	☐ 5:21-43	☐ 6:1-29	☐ 6:30-56	☐ 7:1-23	☐ 7:24-37
15	☐ 8:1-26	☐ 8:27—9:1	☐ 9:2-29	☐ 9:30-50	☐ 10:1-16	☐ 10:17-34	☐ 10:35-52
16	☐ 11:1-16	☐ 11:17-33	☐ 12:1-27	☐ 12:28-44	☐ 13:1-13	☐ 13:14-37	☐ 14:1-26
17	☐ 14:27-52	☐ 14:53-72	☐ 15:1-15	☐ 15:16-47	☐ 16:1-8	☐ 16:9-20	☐ Luke 1:1-4
18	☐ 1:5-25	☐ 1:26-46	☐ 1:47-56	☐ 1:57-80	☐ 2:1-8	☐ 2:9-20	☐ 2:21-39
19	☐ 2:40-52	☐ 3:1-20	☐ 3:21-38	☐ 4:1-13	☐ 4:14-30	☐ 4:31-44	☐ 5:1-26
20	☐ 5:27—6:16	☐ 6:17-38	☐ 6:39-49	☐ 7:1-17	☐ 7:18-23	☐ 7:24-35	☐ 7:36-50
21	☐ 8:1-15	☐ 8:16-25	☐ 8:26-39	☐ 8:40-56	☐ 9:1-17	☐ 9:18-26	☐ 9:27-36
22	☐ 9:37-50	☐ 9:51-62	☐ 10:1-11	☐ 10:12-24	☐ 10:25-37	☐ 10:38-42	☐ 11:1-13
23	☐ 11:14-26	☐ 11:27-36	☐ 11:37-54	☐ 12:1-12	☐ 12:13-21	☐ 12:22-34	☐ 12:35-48
24	☐ 12:49-59	☐ 13:1-9	☐ 13:10-17	☐ 13:18-30	☐ 13:31—14:6	☐ 14:7-14	☐ 14:15-24
25	☐ 14:25-35	☐ 15:1-10	☐ 15:11-21	☐ 15:22-32	☐ 16:1-13	☐ 16:14-22	☐ 16:23-31
26	☐ 17:1-19	☐ 17:20-37	☐ 18:1-14	☐ 18:15-30	☐ 18:31-43	☐ 19:1-10	☐ 19:11-27

Reading Schedule for the Recovery Version of the New Testament with Footnotes

Wk.	Lord's Day	Monday	Tuesday	Wednesday	Thursday	Friday	Saturday
27	☐ Luke 19:28-48	☐ 20:1-19	☐ 20:20-38	☐ 20:39—21:4	☐ 21:5-27	☐ 21:28-38	☐ 22:1-20
28	☐ 22:21-38	☐ 22:39-54	☐ 22:55-71	☐ 23:1-43	☐ 23:44-56	☐ 24:1-12	☐ 24:13-35
29	☐ 24:36-53	☐ John 1:1-13	☐ 1:14-18	☐ 1:19-34	☐ 1:35-51	☐ 2:1-11	☐ 2:12-22
30	☐ 2:23—3:13	☐ 3:14-21	☐ 3:22-36	☐ 4:1-14	☐ 4:15-26	☐ 4:27-42	☐ 4:43-54
31	☐ 5:1-16	☐ 5:17-30	☐ 5:31-47	☐ 6:1-15	☐ 6:16-31	☐ 6:32-51	☐ 6:52-71
32	☐ 7:1-9	☐ 7:10-24	☐ 7:25-36	☐ 7:37-52	☐ 7:53—8:11	☐ 8:12-27	☐ 8:28-44
33	☐ 8:45-59	☐ 9:1-13	☐ 9:14-34	☐ 9:35—10:9	☐ 10:10-30	☐ 10:31—11:4	☐ 11:5-22
34	☐ 11:23-40	☐ 11:41-57	☐ 12:1-11	☐ 12:12-24	☐ 12:25-36	☐ 12:37-50	☐ 13:1-11
35	☐ 13:12-30	☐ 13:31-38	☐ 14:1-6	☐ 14:7-20	☐ 14:21-31	☐ 15:1-11	☐ 15:12-27
36	☐ 16:1-15	☐ 16:16-33	☐ 17:1-5	☐ 17:6-13	☐ 17:14-24	☐ 17:25—18:11	☐ 18:12-27
37	☐ 18:28-40	☐ 19:1-16	☐ 19:17-30	☐ 19:31-42	☐ 20:1-13	☐ 20:14-18	☐ 20:19-22
38	☐ 20:23-31	☐ 21:1-14	☐ 21:15-22	☐ 21:23-25	☐ Acts 1:1-8	☐ 1:9-14	☐ 1:15-26
39	☐ 2:1-13	☐ 2:14-21	☐ 2:22-36	☐ 2:37-41	☐ 2:42-47	☐ 3:1-18	☐ 3:19—4:22
40	☐ 4:23-37	☐ 5:1-16	☐ 5:17-32	☐ 5:33-42	☐ 6:1—7:1	☐ 7:2-29	☐ 7:30-60
41	☐ 8:1-13	☐ 8:14-25	☐ 8:26-40	☐ 9:1-19	☐ 9:20-43	☐ 10:1-16	☐ 10:17-33
42	☐ 10:34-48	☐ 11:1-18	☐ 11:19-30	☐ 12:1-25	☐ 13:1-12	☐ 13:13-43	☐ 13:44—14:5
43	☐ 14:6-28	☐ 15:1-12	☐ 15:13-34	☐ 15:35—16:5	☐ 16:6-18	☐ 16:19-40	☐ 17:1-18
44	☐ 17:19-34	☐ 18:1-17	☐ 18:18-28	☐ 19:1-20	☐ 19:21-41	☐ 20:1-12	☐ 20:13-38
45	☐ 21:1-14	☐ 21:15-26	☐ 21:27-40	☐ 22:1-21	☐ 22:22-29	☐ 22:30—23:11	☐ 23:12-15
46	☐ 23:16-30	☐ 23:31—24:21	☐ 24:22—25:5	☐ 25:6-27	☐ 26:1-13	☐ 26:14-32	☐ 27:1-26
47	☐ 27:27—28:10	☐ 28:11-22	☐ 28:23-31	☐ Rom 1:1-2	☐ 1:3-7	☐ 1:8-17	☐ 1:18-25
48	☐ 1:26—2:10	☐ 2:11-29	☐ 3:1-20	☐ 3:21-31	☐ 4:1-12	☐ 4:13-25	☐ 5:1-11
49	☐ 5:12-17	☐ 5:18—6:5	☐ 6:6-11	☐ 6:12-23	☐ 7:1-12	☐ 7:13-25	☐ 8:1-2
50	☐ 8:3-6	☐ 8:7-13	☐ 8:14-25	☐ 8:26-39	☐ 9:1-18	☐ 9:19—10:3	☐ 10:4-15
51	☐ 10:16—11:10	☐ 11:11-22	☐ 11:23-36	☐ 12:1-3	☐ 12:4-21	☐ 13:1-14	☐ 14:1-12
52	☐ 14:13-23	☐ 15:1-13	☐ 15:14-33	☐ 16:1-5	☐ 16:6-24	☐ 16:25-27	☐ I Cor 1:1-4

Reading Schedule for the Recovery Version of the New Testament with Footnotes

Wk.	Lord's Day	Monday	Tuesday	Wednesday	Thursday	Friday	Saturday
53	☐ I Cor 1:5-9	☐ 1:10-17	☐ 1:18-31	☐ 2:1-5	☐ 2:6-10	☐ 2:11-16	☐ 3:1-9
54	☐ 3:10-13	☐ 3:14-23	☐ 4:1-9	☐ 4:10-21	☐ 5:1-13	☐ 6:1-11	☐ 6:12-20
55	☐ 7:1-16	☐ 7:17-24	☐ 7:25-40	☐ 8:1-13	☐ 9:1-15	☐ 9:16-27	☐ 10:1-4
56	☐ 10:5-13	☐ 10:14-33	☐ 11:1-6	☐ 11:7-16	☐ 11:17-26	☐ 11:27-34	☐ 12:1-11
57	☐ 12:12-22	☐ 12:23-31	☐ 13:1-13	☐ 14:1-12	☐ 14:13-25	☐ 14:26-33	☐ 14:34-40
58	☐ 15:1-19	☐ 15:20-28	☐ 15:29-34	☐ 15:35-49	☐ 15:50-58	☐ 16:1-9	☐ 16:10-24
59	☐ II Cor 1:1-4	☐ 1:5-14	☐ 1:15-22	☐ 1:23—2:11	☐ 2:12-17	☐ 3:1-6	☐ 3:7-11
60	☐ 3:12-18	☐ 4:1-6	☐ 4:7-12	☐ 4:13-18	☐ 5:1-8	☐ 5:9-15	☐ 5:16-21
61	☐ 6:1-13	☐ 6:14—7:4	☐ 7:5-16	☐ 8:1-15	☐ 8:16-24	☐ 9:1-15	☐ 10:1-6
62	☐ 10:7-18	☐ 11:1-15	☐ 11:16-33	☐ 12:1-10	☐ 12:11-21	☐ 13:1-10	☐ 13:11-14
63	☐ Gal 1:1-5	☐ 1:6-14	☐ 1:15-24	☐ 2:1-13	☐ 2:14-21	☐ 3:1-4	☐ 3:5-14
64	☐ 3:15-22	☐ 3:23-29	☐ 4:1-7	☐ 4:8-20	☐ 4:21-31	☐ 5:1-12	☐ 5:13-21
65	☐ 5:22-26	☐ 6:1-10	☐ 6:11-15	☐ 6:16-18	☐ Eph 1:1-3	☐ 1:4-6	☐ 1:7-10
66	☐ 1:11-14	☐ 1:15-18	☐ 1:19-23	☐ 2:1-5	☐ 2:6-10	☐ 2:11-14	☐ 2:15-18
67	☐ 2:19-22	☐ 3:1-7	☐ 3:8-13	☐ 3:14-18	☐ 3:19-21	☐ 4:1-4	☐ 4:5-10
68	☐ 4:11-16	☐ 4:17-24	☐ 4:25-32	☐ 5:1-10	☐ 5:11-21	☐ 5:22-26	☐ 5:27-33
69	☐ 6:1-9	☐ 6:10-14	☐ 6:15-18	☐ 6:19-24	☐ Phil 1:1-7	☐ 1:8-18	☐ 1:19-26
70	☐ 1:27—2:4	☐ 2:5-11	☐ 2:12-16	☐ 2:17-30	☐ 3:1-6	☐ 3:7-11	☐ 3:12-16
71	☐ 3:17-21	☐ 4:1-9	☐ 4:10-23	☐ Col 1:1-8	☐ 1:9-13	☐ 1:14-23	☐ 1:24-29
72	☐ 2:1-7	☐ 2:8-15	☐ 2:16-23	☐ 3:1-4	☐ 3:5-15	☐ 3:16-25	☐ 4:1-18
73	☐ I Thes 1:1-3	☐ 1:4-10	☐ 2:1-12	☐ 2:13—3:5	☐ 3:6-13	☐ 4:1-10	☐ 4:11—5:11
74	☐ 5:12-28	☐ II Thes 1:1-12	☐ 2:1-17	☐ 3:1-18	☐ I Tim 1:1-2	☐ 1:3-4	☐ 1:5-14
75	☐ 1:15-20	☐ 2:1-7	☐ 2:8-15	☐ 3:1-13	☐ 3:14—4:5	☐ 4:6-16	☐ 5:1-25
76	☐ 6:1-10	☐ 6:11-21	☐ II Tim 1:1-10	☐ 1:11-18	☐ 2:1-15	☐ 2:16-26	☐ 3:1-13
77	☐ 3:14—4:8	☐ 4:9-22	☐ Titus 1:1-4	☐ 1:5-16	☐ 2:1-15	☐ 3:1-8	☐ 3:9-15
78	☐ Philem 1:1-11	☐ 1:12-25	☐ Heb 1:1-2	☐ 1:3-5	☐ 1:6-14	☐ 2:1-9	☐ 2:10-18

Reading Schedule for the Recovery Version of the New Testament with Footnotes

Wk.	Lord's Day	Monday	Tuesday	Wednesday	Thursday	Friday	Saturday
79	Heb 3:1-6	3:7-19	4:1-9	4:10-13	4:14-16	5:1-10	5:11—6:3
80	6:4-8	6:9-20	7:1-10	7:11-28	8:1-6	8:7-13	9:1-4
81	9:5-14	9:15-28	10:1-18	10:19-28	10:29-39	11:1-6	11:7-19
82	11:20-31	11:32-40	12:1-2	12:3-13	12:14-17	12:18-26	12:27-29
83	13:1-7	13:8-12	13:13-15	13:16-25	James 1:1-8	1:9-18	1:19-27
84	2:1-13	2:14-26	3:1-18	4:1-10	4:11-17	5:1-12	5:13-20
85	I Pet 1:1-2	1:3-4	1:5	1:6-9	1:10-12	1:13-17	1:18-25
86	2:1-3	2:4-8	2:9-17	2:18-25	3:1-13	3:14-22	4:1-6
87	4:7-16	4:17-19	5:1-4	5:5-9	5:10-14	II Pet 1:1-2	1:3-4
88	1:5-8	1:9-11	1:12-18	1:19-21	2:1-3	2:4-11	2:12-22
89	3:1-6	3:7-9	3:10-12	3:13-15	3:16	3:17-18	I John 1:1-2
90	1:3-4	1:5	1:6	1:7	1:8-10	2:1-2	2:3-11
91	2:12-14	2:15-19	2:20-23	2:24-27	2:28-29	3:1-5	3:6-10
92	3:11-18	3:19-24	4:1-6	4:7-11	4:12-15	4:16—5:3	5:4-13
93	5:14-17	5:18-21	II John 1:1-3	1:4-9	1:10-13	III John 1:1-6	1:7-14
94	Jude 1:1-4	1:5-10	1:11-19	1:20-25	Rev 1:1-3	1:4-6	1:7-11
95	1:12-13	1:14-16	1:17-20	2:1-6	2:7	2:8-9	2:10-11
96	2:12-14	2:15-17	2:18-23	2:24-29	3:1-3	3:4-6	3:7-9
97	3:10-13	3:14-18	3:19-22	4:1-5	4:6-7	4:8-11	5:1-6
98	5:7-14	6:1-8	6:9-17	7:1-8	7:9-17	8:1-6	8:7-12
99	8:13—9:11	9:12-21	10:1-4	10:5-11	11:1-4	11:5-14	11:15-19
100	12:1-4	12:5-9	12:10-18	13:1-10	13:11-18	14:1-5	14:6-12
101	14:13-20	15:1-8	16:1-12	16:13-21	17:1-6	17:7-18	18:1-8
102	18:9—19:4	19:5-10	19:11-16	19:17-21	20:1-6	20:7-10	20:11-15
103	21:1	21:2	21:3-8	21:9-13	21:14-18	21:19-21	21:22-27
104	22:1	22:2	22:3-11	22:12-15	22:16-17	22:18-21	

Week 1 - Day 4 — Today's verses

1 Tim. 1:5 But the end of the charge is love out of a pure heart and out of a good conscience and out of unfeigned faith.

Titus 1:15 All things are pure to the pure; yet to those who are defiled and unbelieving nothing is pure, but both their mind and their conscience are defiled.

Date

Week 1 - Day 5 — Today's verses

2 Cor. 6:4, 6 ...In everything we commend ourselves as ministers of God...in pureness, in knowledge, in long-suffering, in kindness, in a holy spirit, in unfeigned love.

Heb. 4:12 For the word of God is living and operative and sharper than any two-edged sword, and piercing even to the dividing of soul and spirit...and able to discern the thoughts and intentions of the heart.

Date

Week 1 - Day 6 — Today's verses

2 Cor. 5:21 Him who did not know sin on our behalf that we might become the righteousness of God in Him.

Rev. 1:20 The mystery of...the seven golden lampstands:... The seven lampstands are the seven churches.

21:18 ...And the city was pure gold, like clear glass.

22:1 And he showed me a river of water of life, bright as crystal, proceeding out of the throne of God and of the Lamb in the middle of its street.

Date

Week 1 - Day 1 — Today's verses

Eph. 3:16 That He would grant you...to be strengthened with power through His Spirit into the inner man.

4:22 That you put off, as regards your former manner of life, the old man, which is being corrupted...

24 And put on the new man, which was created according to God in righteousness and holiness of the reality.

1 Cor. 2:14 ...A soulish man does not receive the things of the Spirit of God, for they are foolishness to him and he is not able to know them because they are discerned spiritually.

Date

Week 1 - Day 2 — Today's verses

Heb. 4:12 For the word of God is living and operative and sharper than any two-edged sword, and piercing even to the dividing of soul and spirit and of joints and marrow, and able to discern the thoughts and intentions of the heart.

2 Cor. 7:1 Therefore since we have these promises, beloved, let us cleanse ourselves from all defilement of flesh and of spirit, perfecting holiness in the fear of God.

1 Thes. 5:23 And the God of peace Himself sanctify you wholly, and may your spirit and soul and body be preserved complete, without blame, at the coming of our Lord Jesus Christ.

Date

Week 1 - Day 3 — Today's verses

Acts 23:1 And Paul...said, Men, brothers, I have conducted myself in all good conscience before God until this day.

24:16 Because of this I also exercise myself to always have a conscience without offense toward God and men.

2 Tim. 1:3 I thank God, whom I serve from my forefathers in a pure conscience....

1 Tim. 3:9 Holding the mystery of the faith in a pure conscience.

Date

Week 2 - Day 4   Today's verses

1 Tim. ...Our Savior God, who desires all men to
2:3-4 be saved and to come to the full knowledge of the truth.

Col. Let the word of Christ dwell in you richly
3:16 in all wisdom, teaching and admonishing
one another...

1 Tim. If you lay these things before the brothers,
4:6 you will be a good minister of Christ Jesus, being nourished with the words of
the faith and of the good teaching which
you have closely followed.

_____
Date

Week 2 - Day 5   Today's verses

Eph. And for me, that utterance may be given
6:19 to me in the opening of my mouth, to
make known in boldness the mystery of
the gospel.

1 Cor. Which things also we speak, not in words
2:13 taught by human wisdom but in words
taught by the Spirit, interpreting spiritual
things with spiritual *words*.

_____
Date

Week 2 - Day 6   Today's verses

2 Tim. Be diligent to present yourself approved
2:15 to God, an unashamed workman, cutting
straight the word of the truth.

Neh. And on the second day the heads of fa-
8:13 thers' *houses* of all the people, the priests,
and the Levites were gathered to Ezra the
scribe, that is, in order to gain insight into
the words of the law.

_____
Date

Week 2 - Day 1   Today's verses

Col. ...The Son of His love,...who is the image
1:13, 15 of the invisible God...

Phil. According to my earnest expectation and
1:20-21 hope that in nothing I will be put to
shame, but with all boldness, as always,
even now Christ will be magnified in my
body, whether through life or through
death. For to me, to live is Christ...

_____
Date

Week 2 - Day 2   Today's verses

2 Tim. And the things which you have heard
2:2 from me through many witnesses, these
commit to faithful men, who will be competent to teach others also.

1 Tim. ...*I* write that you may know how one
3:15 ought to conduct himself in the house of
God, which is the church of the living
God, the pillar and base of the truth.

2 Pet. Therefore I will be ready always to remind
1:12 you concerning these things, even though
you know *them* and have been established in the present truth.

_____
Date

Week 2 - Day 3   Today's verses

Eph. That by revelation the mystery was made
3:3-4 known to me, as I have written previously
in brief, by which, in reading *it*, you can
perceive my understanding in the mystery
of Christ.

9 And to enlighten all *that they may see*
what the economy of the mystery is,
which throughout the ages has been hidden in God, who created all things.

2 Tim. For which I was appointed a herald and
1:11 an apostle and a teacher.

3:16 All Scripture is God-breathed and profitable for teaching, for conviction, for correction, for instruction in righteousness.

_____
Date

Week 3 - Day 4   Today's verses

1 Cor. 2:14 But a soulish man does not receive the things of the Spirit of God, for they are foolishness to him and he is not able to know *them* because they are discerned spiritually.

Phil. 3:3 For we are the circumcision, the ones who serve by the Spirit of God and boast in Christ Jesus and have no confidence in the flesh.

7 But what things were gains to me, these I have counted as loss on account of Christ.

_____
Date

Week 3 - Day 1   Today's verses

Psa. 36:8-9 They are saturated with the fatness of Your house, and You cause them to drink of the river of Your pleasures. For with You is the fountain of life; in Your light we see light.

2 Tim. 2:15 Be diligent to present yourself approved to God, an unashamed workman, cutting straight the word of the truth.

Acts 26:19 ...I was not disobedient to the heavenly vision.

_____
Date

Week 3 - Day 5   Today's verses

Eph. 4:4-6 One Body and one Spirit, even as also you were called in one hope of your calling; one Lord, one faith, one baptism; one God and Father of all, who is over all and through all and in all.

_____
Date

Week 3 - Day 2   Today's verses

Eph. 3:16-17 That He would grant you, according to the riches of His glory, to be strengthened with power through His Spirit into the inner man, that Christ may make His home in your hearts through faith...

19 ...That you may be filled unto all the fullness of God.

_____
Date

Week 3 - Day 6   Today's verses

Gal. 3:27-28 For as many of you as were baptized into Christ have put on Christ. There cannot be Jew nor Greek, there cannot be slave nor free man, there cannot be male and female; for you are all one in Christ Jesus.

Col. 3:10-11 And have put on the new man, which is being renewed unto full knowledge according to the image of Him who created him, where there cannot be Greek and Jew, circumcision and uncircumcision, barbarian, Scythian, slave, free man, but Christ is all and in all.

_____
Date

Week 3 - Day 3   Today's verses

Exo. 16:15 ...And Moses said to them, It is the bread which Jehovah has given you to eat.

John 6:27 Work not for the food which perishes, but for the food which abides unto eternal life, which the Son of Man will give you...

35 Jesus said to them, I am the bread of life; he who comes to Me shall by no means hunger, and he who believes into Me shall by no means ever thirst.

_____
Date

Week 4 - Day 4 — Today's verses

Exo. 1:11 So they set taskmasters over them to afflict them with their burdens. And they built storage cities for Pharaoh, Pithom and Raamses.

Rom. 12:1-2 I exhort you therefore, brothers, through the compassions of God to present your bodies a living sacrifice, holy, well pleasing to God, which is your reasonable service. And do not be fashioned according to this age, but be transformed by the renewing of the mind that you may prove what the will of God is, that which is good and well pleasing and perfect.

_____
Date

Week 4 - Day 5 — Today's verses

Luke 17:32-33 Remember Lot's wife. Whoever seeks to preserve his soul-life will lose it, and whoever loses it will preserve it alive.

1 John 2:28 And now, little children, abide in Him, so that if He is manifested, we may have boldness and not be put to shame from Him at His coming.

_____
Date

Week 4 - Day 6 — Today's verses

1 John 5:4 For everything that has been begotten of God overcomes the world; and this is the victory which has overcome the world—our faith.

18-19 We know that everyone who is begotten of God does not sin, but he who has been begotten of God keeps himself, and the evil one does not touch him. We know that we are of God, and the whole world lies in the evil one.

21 Little children, guard yourselves from idols.

_____
Date

Week 4 - Day 1 — Today's verses

Neh. 2:17 ...Come and let us build up the wall of Jerusalem so that we will no longer be a reproach.

Rev. 21:10, 12 And he...showed me the holy city, Jerusalem, coming down out of heaven from God....It had a great and high wall...

18-19 And the building work of its wall was jasper....The foundations of the wall of the city were adorned with every precious stone....

2 Cor. 3:18 But we all with unveiled face, beholding and reflecting like a mirror the glory of the Lord, are being transformed into the same image from glory to glory, even as from the Lord Spirit.

_____
Date

Week 4 - Day 2 — Today's verses

1 John 2:15, 17 Do not love the world nor the things in the world.... And the world is passing away, and its lust; but he who does the will of God abides forever.

Matt. 6:31-33 Therefore do not be anxious, saying, What shall we eat? or, What shall we drink? or, With what shall we be clothed? For all these things the Gentiles are anxiously seeking. For your heavenly Father knows that you need all these things. But seek first His kingdom and His righteousness, and all these things will be added to you.

_____
Date

Week 4 - Day 3 — Today's verses

Luke 12:21 So is he who stores up treasure for himself and is not rich toward God.

2 Tim. 3:2, 4 For men will be lovers of self, lovers of money, boasters, arrogant, revilers, disobedient to parents, unthankful, unholy,...traitors, reckless, blinded with pride, lovers of pleasure rather than lovers of God.

1 John 5:21 Little children, guard yourselves from idols.

_____
Date

Week 5 - Day 4 — Today's verses

Rom. Now the God of peace will crush Satan
16:20 under your feet shortly. The grace of our
Lord Jesus be with you.

Eph. Put on the whole armor of God that you
6:11 may be able to stand against the stratagems of the devil.

16-17 Besides all these, having taken up the
shield of faith, with which you will be
able to quench all the flaming darts of the
evil one. And receive the helmet of salvation and the sword of the Spirit, which
Spirit is the word of God.

_____
Date

Week 5 - Day 5 — Today's verses

Dan. And he will speak things against the Most
7:25 High and wear out the saints of the Most
High...

2 Thes. But the Lord is faithful, who will establish
3:3 you and guard you from the evil one.

Rev. And they overcame him because of the
12:11 blood of the Lamb and because of the
word of their testimony...

Eph. Therefore take up the whole armor of God
6:13 that you may be able to withstand in the
evil day, and having done all, to stand.

_____
Date

Week 5 - Day 6 — Today's verses

Eph. And raised us up together with Him and
2:6 seated us together with Him in the
heavenlies in Christ Jesus.

6:12 For our wrestling is not against blood and
flesh but against the rulers, against the authorities, against the world-rulers of this
darkness, against the spiritual forces of
evil in the heavenlies.

2 Tim. No one serving as a soldier entangles
2:4 himself with the affairs of this life, that he
may please the one who enlisted him.

4:7 I have fought the good fight; I have finished the course; I have kept the faith.

_____
Date

Week 5 - Day 1 — Today's verses

Neh. ...Come and let us build up the wall of Je-
2:17 rusalem so that we will no longer be a reproach.

Rom. For the kingdom of God is not eating and
14:17 drinking, but righteousness and peace
and joy in the Holy Spirit.

Rev. ...And the throne of God and of the Lamb
22:3 will be in it...

_____
Date

Week 5 - Day 2 — Today's verses

S. S. Oh, you are beautiful, my love! Oh, you
4:1 are beautiful! Your eyes are like doves behind your veil; your hair is like a flock of
goats that repose on Mount Gilead.

4 Your neck is like the tower of David, built
for an armory: a thousand bucklers hang
on it, all the shields of the mighty men.

7:4 Your neck is like a tower of ivory; your
eyes, like the pools in Heshbon by the
gate of Bath-rabbim; your nose is like the
tower of Lebanon, which faces Damascus.

_____
Date

Week 5 - Day 3 — Today's verses

Num. ...When a man or a woman makes a spe-
6:2 cial vow, the vow of a Nazarite, to separate himself to Jehovah.

5 All the days of his vow of separation no razor shall pass over his head. He shall be
holy until the days are fulfilled for which
he separated himself to Jehovah; he shall
let the locks of the hair of his head grow
long.

Col. And He is the Head of the Body, the
1:18 church; He is the beginning, the Firstborn
from the dead, that He Himself might
have the first place in all things.

_____
Date

Week 6 - Day 4 — Today's verses

Josh. 18:1 And the whole assembly of the children of Israel gathered together at Shiloh, and they set up the Tent of Meeting there; and the land was subdued before them.

2 Sam. 6:12 And it was told King David, saying, Jehovah has blessed the house of Obed-edom and all that he has because of the Ark of God. So David went and brought up the Ark of God from the house of Obed-edom into the city of David with rejoicing.

1 Kings 8:13 I have surely built You a lofty house, a place for You to dwell in forever.

Date _____

Week 6 - Day 5 — Today's verses

1 Kings 11:7-8 Then Solomon built a high place to Chemosh the detestable thing of Moab in the mountain that is before Jerusalem and to Molech the detestable thing of the children of Ammon. And so he did for all his foreign wives, who burned incense and offered sacrifices to their gods.

2 Chron. 36:18-19 And all the vessels of the house of God, great and small, and the treasures of the house of Jehovah and the treasures of the king and of his princes, all these he brought to Babylon. And they burned down the house of God; and they broke down the wall of Jerusalem and burned down all its palaces with fire, and all its precious vessels were given up to destruction.

Date _____

Week 6 - Day 6 — Today's verses

Rev. 4:3 And He who was sitting was like a jasper stone...in appearance...

21:10-11 And he carried me away in spirit onto a great and high mountain and showed me the holy city, Jerusalem, coming down out of heaven from God, having the glory of God. Her light was like a most precious stone, like a jasper stone, as clear as crystal.

18 And the building work of its wall was jasper...

Date _____

Week 6 - Day 1 — Today's verses

Gen. 1:26 And God said, Let Us make man in Our image, according to Our likeness; and let them have dominion...

2:9 And out of the ground Jehovah God caused to grow every tree that is pleasant to the sight and good for food, as well as the tree of life in the middle of the garden...

1 Kings 8:11 And the priests were not able to stand and minister because of the cloud, for the glory of Jehovah filled the house of Jehovah.

Date _____

Week 6 - Day 2 — Today's verses

John 1:14 And the Word became flesh and tabernacled among us (and we beheld His glory, glory as of the only Begotten from the Father), full of grace and reality.

Eph. 2:22 In whom you also are being built together into a dwelling place of God in spirit.

1 Tim. 3:15-16 ...The house of God, which is the church of the living God, the pillar and base of the truth. And confessedly, great is the mystery of godliness: He who was manifested in the flesh...

Date _____

Week 6 - Day 3 — Today's verses

Exo. 25:16 And you shall put into the Ark the Testimony which I shall give you.

40:35 And Moses was not able to enter the Tent of Meeting, because the cloud settled on it and the glory of Jehovah filled the tabernacle.

Rev. 21:10-11 And he...showed me the holy city, Jerusalem, coming down out of heaven from God, having the glory of God...

Date _____